BOTS &
BRILLIANCE

BOTS &
BRILLIANCE

101 THINGS
YOU SHOULD KNOW ABOUT ARTIFICIAL INTELLIGENCE

JOHN BINKS

Bots & Brilliance: 101 Things You Should Know About Artificial Intelligence

Printed in the United States of America
First Edition 2024
CIP data for this book is available at the Library of Congress.

For more information, email John@BotsAndBosses.com.

www.BotsAndBosses.com

ISBN: 9798879251692

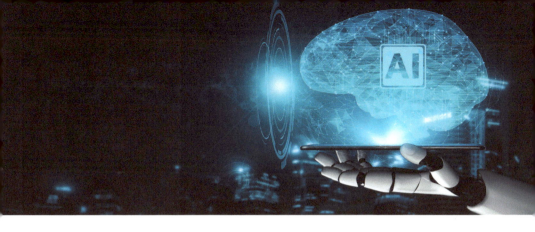

TABLE OF CONTENTS

FOREWORD
CHARTING THE COURSE THROUGH THE AI ODYSSEY

In an era where the boundaries between the possible and the impossible are constantly being redrawn, *"Bots & Brilliance: 101 Things You Should Know About Artificial Intelligence"* emerges as a beacon, illuminating the vast and often mystifying landscape of Artificial Intelligence (AI). As we stand on the cusp of a technological revolution, where AI is not just an innovation but a fundamental shift in our interaction with technology, this book serves as an essential guide, a compass to navigate the complex world of AI.

The journey into AI is much like exploring a new continent. It's vast, diverse, and rich in potential. But it can also be daunting. Where does one start? What are the key landmarks? How does one make sense of the intricate details and the overarching patterns? "Bots & Brilliance" answers these questions and more, offering a comprehensive yet accessible exploration of AI.

The author of this book has meticulously crafted an informative and engaging narrative, ensuring that the content resonates with professionals, enthusiasts, and beginners alike. Each chapter blends depth and clarity, presenting AI concepts, their applications, and implications with precision and insight. The book doesn't just inform; it inspires, urging the reader to consider the broader implications of AI on society, ethics, and the future.

As you delve into the pages of this book, you will encounter a range of topics, from the fundamentals of machine learning to the ethical considerations of AI deployment. You will read about the transformative impact of AI across industries, the evolving nature of work in an AI-driven world, and the critical role of AI in addressing global challenges. Each chapter is a piece of the puzzle, and as you progress, a comprehensive picture of AI emerges.

"Bots & Brilliance" is more than just a book; it's a journey into the heart of AI. It's an odyssey that takes you from the roots of AI's history to the peaks of its future possibilities. As you embark on this journey, be prepared to be challenged, enlightened, and inspired. AI has endless possibilities and profound questions; this book is your guide.

Welcome to "Bots & Brilliance." The journey into the world of AI starts here.

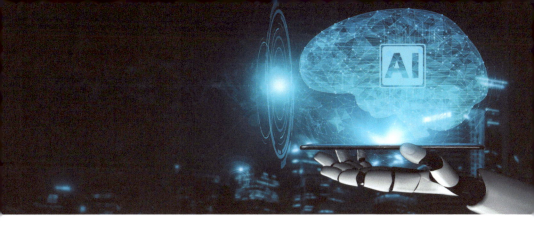

INTRODUCTION

Welcome to "Bots & Brilliance," a captivating expedition into the world of Artificial Intelligence (AI), a domain where machines don't just compute but learn, adapt, and sometimes, even surprise us. This book is a mosaic of insights, spanning from the foundational concepts of AI to its profound impact on our daily lives, workplaces, ethical considerations, and beyond. Whether you're a curious newcomer, a tech enthusiast, or someone navigating the changing landscapes of various professions, this book aims to enlighten, inform, and inspire.

Our journey begins with "AI, A Love Story" (Chapter 1), where we introduce AI not as a cold, calculating machine but as a dynamic and evolving field. Think of AI as a super-smart parrot capable of mimicking, learning, and occasionally talking back. We'll traverse the rich history of AI and its comparison with the human brain and delve into the nuts and bolts of machine learning, deep learning, and neural networks. This chapter sets the stage by demystifying the algorithms and data that are the lifeblood of AI.

"AI for the Complete Beginner" (Chapter 2) demystifies AI for those just starting their journey. It debunks common AI myths, suggests simple experiments, and helps understand AI news and concepts without jargon. It's a gentle introduction to the world of AI, emphasizing its limitations and the importance of human oversight.

As we step into "AI in Your Daily Life" (Chapter 3), you'll see how AI is no longer a futuristic fantasy but a present reality. AI's invisible hand is ever-present, from the smartphone in your pocket to how social media algorithms curate your feed. We'll explore its role in entertainment, e-commerce, smart homes, healthcare, and more, revealing how AI is intricately woven into the fabric of our everyday existence.

"AI at Work" (Chapter 4) focuses on the professional sphere. Here, we delve into AI's transformative role across various industries. From streamlining business processes to revolutionizing fields like agriculture, marketing, and customer service, AI redefines efficiency and innovation. This chapter also addresses the growing significance of AI in creative domains, challenging the traditional boundaries between technology and art.

For the enthusiasts and practitioners, "AI for the Tech Enthusiast" (Chapter 5) offers a deep dive into building AI projects, understanding the jargon, and staying abreast of emerging technologies. It's a chapter that celebrates the collaborative spirit of the AI community and its role in addressing global challenges.

In "AI for the Non-Tech Professional" (Chapter 6), we explore AI's impact on law, real estate, journalism, and education. This chapter is a testament to AI's far-reaching implications beyond the tech world, offering insights into how professionals can adapt and thrive in an AI-augmented landscape.

However, it's not all bright and shiny. "The Dark Side of AI" (Chapter 7) confronts AI's challenges and ethical dilemmas. We discuss the biases inherent in AI systems, privacy concerns, the potential for job displacement, and the controversial use of AI in warfare. The "The AI Singularity" section invites readers to ponder the future implications of AI surpassing human intelligence.

Looking ahead, "The Future of AI" (Chapter 8) depicts possibilities and challenges. From AI's role in space exploration and quantum computing to its potential in addressing sustainability, this chapter encourages readers to think about the ethical dimensions of AI and the global race to harness its power.

"AI and Management" (Chapter 9) delves into how AI reshapes leadership and decision-making in the corporate world. It discusses AI's role in business strategy, employee training, and even corporate governance, providing a roadmap for managers and leaders to integrate AI into their systems.

"The Manager's Perspective" (Chapter 10) invites readers to walk in the shoes of managers exploring the exciting realm of AI in the workplace. Envision this chapter as the quintessential 'Manager's Guide to AI,' but more engaging and lighter in tone, devoid of tedious lectures and sprinkled with humor. It's tailored for leaders, decision-makers, and anyone who has ever pondered, "I'm leading a team, and suddenly there's AI in the mix. What do I do now?"

"Personal Anecdotes and Insights" (Chapter 11) brings a human touch to the AI narrative. It's a collection of personal experiences, humorous blunders, and success stories that highlight the human aspect of AI, reminding us that behind every algorithm is a team of dedicated individuals.

As we conclude with "Embracing AI: A Call to Action" (Conclusion), we invite you to view AI not just as a technological force but as a tool that, when wielded wisely, can bring about unprecedented advancements and solutions to complex problems.

In the epilogue, we reflect on the journey through "Bots & Brilliance." Remember, like any tool, AI demonstrates the brilliance or flaws of those who harness it. Whether you're a tech enthusiast, a beginner, or a non-tech professional, the future of AI is intertwined with your actions and decisions. So, let's embark on this journey together and shape a future where AI is not just about intelligent machines but about the wisdom, ethics, and creativity of those who guide them.

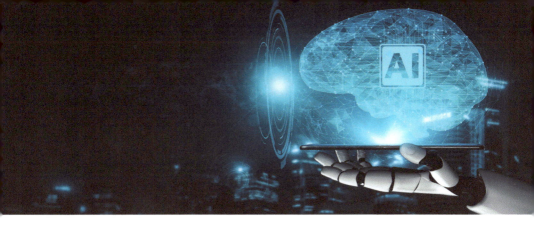

CHAPTER I
AI, A LOVE STORY

Chapter 1, "AI, A Love Story," is where our enchanting romance with Artificial Intelligence (AI) begins. Think of it as a first date with AI, where we get to know each other over a candlelit dinner, except the candles are just the glowing screens of our devices. This chapter demystifies AI, breaking it down from a towering concept into something as approachable as a friendly robot in a sci-fi movie.

We start by answering the burning question: What is AI? Imagine a super-smart parrot that mimics and learns from what it hears. That's AI– a blend of brilliance and occasional cheekiness. We then stroll down memory lane, exploring AI's history, which is more dramatic than most TV series, featuring ancient automata, chess-playing computers, and the occasional winter (but without the snow).

Next, we pit AI against the human brain in a friendly match of wits. Spoiler alert: AI can process faster than a caffeinated supercomputer, but don't expect it to write poetry about the sunset. We dive into the world of machine learning, which is like teaching a child to cook – it's messy, but the results can be surprisingly delightful (or at least edible).

Deep learning gets a spotlight, too, where AI starts dreaming of electric sheep and other complex things. Neural networks are up next, and we explain them as a million tiny brains working on your math homework so you don't have to.

Algorithms, the secret sauce of AI, are demystified next. They're like mysterious recipes that AI chefs use to whip up everything from your online shopping recommendations to predicting the weather. Data, the food for AI, is discussed with an emphasis on quality over quantity because no one likes a half-baked AI.

We wrap up the chapter with a look at different learning methods in AI, comparing supervised and unsupervised learning to other parenting styles and reinforcement learning to the school of hard knocks.

"AI, A Love Story" is your ticket to understanding AI without needing a PhD in computer science. It's a chapter that says, "Hey, AI might seem complex, but let's have some fun while we figure it out together." So, grab your favorite snack, make yourself comfortable, and start this AI love story with humor, facts, and maybe some magic.

1. **What is AI?** - Artificial Intelligence (AI) is a branch of computer science that seeks to build intelligent machines capable of working and reacting like humans. In other words, these machines are designed to do things that usually require human intelligence, such as visual perception, speech recognition, decision-making, and language translation. The unique thing about AI is its ability to rationalize and take action with the highest chance of achieving a specific goal. It's like having a digital mind with the ability to think, analyze, and decide.

There are two primary types of AI we've come up with so far: Narrow AI and General AI. Narrow AI is trained for specific tasks, such as voice recognition systems or internet searches (how Siri or

Google can understand our commands). At the same time, General AI is more similar to human intelligence in terms of being able to perform any intellectual task a human can do. We don't have many examples of this type, but when developed, it would enable machines to think and solve problems just like us.

Currently, AI applications can be found almost anywhere you look. We're encountering them daily, and the list keeps growing. For example, in manufacturing, predictive maintenance powered by AI is becoming increasingly popular, making it possible to prevent equipment failures from happening in the first place. Autonomous vehicles are another one — they rely heavily on AI for quick decision-making in traffic situations.

One more notable application of AI lies within the healthcare industry. Do you know those images your doctor takes during a check-up? Well, now they're putting them through an algorithm powered by AI, which achieves incredible accuracy when processing and analyzing them. For example, it's been shown that when detecting diabetic retinopathy (an eye disease caused by diabetes), an algorithm could achieve diagnoses as accurate as those made by humans — if not more precise— all while being way faster at it, too.

The influence of AI is everywhere around us — simplifying things and opening up new doors in technology. The speed and rate at which AI is evolving is genuinely unique and gives us a glimpse of what the future might look like when machines help us with our everyday tasks and assist in solving the most challenging problems we face.

2. **History of AI -** Artificial Intelligence (AI) is pretty crazy. It's not new; you can find it in ancient myths and legends about mechanical men and automata! These tales reflect our undying fascination with trying to create intelligent beings. However, the AI we know today started to take shape in the mid-20th century.

A British mathematician and computer scientist, Alan Turing, played a significant role. He came up with the Turing Test, which builds a criterion for machine intelligence. In his test, if a machine could hold a conversation with a human without the human realizing it's talking to the device, then it's considered intelligent. This concept fundamentally challenged our understanding of both machine capabilities and the nature of intelligence.

Another big moment was the Dartmouth Conference in 1956. That meeting is generally known as the birth of AI as we understand it now. The brains at the time set very ambitious goals, but they were necessary to get things going.

One of AI's earliest achievements was by Joseph Weizenbaum in the 1960s, creating ELIZA, an early natural language processing computer program. The cool part about ELIZA was that it could mimic human conversation by recognizing specific keywords and responding with pre-programmed scripts. Although primitive, ELIZA demonstrated that AI could read our language like we do, thus sparking further interest and investment in the field.

Fast forward to now, and our creations have evolved far beyond what their creators thought imaginable. They've learned how to learn and gotten good at it, too! An example is Google's DeepMind with its program AlphaGo, which managed to beat Lee Sedol, a world champion in Go, making headlines worldwide.

We watch these developments happen daily, and one thing becomes increasingly clear: AI is not just another advancement for us. It represents our thirst for knowledge on how we can replicate ours or, better yet, surpass our abilities!

3. **AI vs. Human Brain** - Indeed, the human brain and AI each have unique differences and similarities. AI, most noticeably with machine learning, can quickly process large amounts of data. It can even perform tasks at an efficient pace that humans would never be able to match. This ability alone has made it a powerful tool across many fields.

However, despite its impressive capabilities, AI lacks certain qualities that make humans unique. Emotional intelligence, ethical reasoning, and creative thought are all things that AI does not have. IBM's WatsonX, for example, is known for its ability to analyze vast amounts of data but cannot empathize with patients or make ethical decisions.

This isn't to say that AI won't eventually be able to do these things. But as it stands now, it's pretty clear that there is still a significant gap between AI and the human brain. Based on our knowledge, AI is excellent at analyzing and performing tasks but falls short in understanding emotions and ethical considerations.

With more companies recognizing these limitations daily, efforts have been redirected toward bridging some gaps. In particular, Affectiva's emotion recognition technology looks promising. This technology explicitly blends AI's analytical power with a deeper understanding of human emotions. While at first, this may sound like something out of a Sci-fi movie... "What's next? They're going to want to be just like us!" The goal here isn't to create robots with emotions but to allow machines to understand why people may feel a certain way so they can respond gently.

Developing a more empathetic machine isn't just some technical challenge; doing so pushes scientists and engineers to ponder "What makes us human?" How far are we willing to try the limits until something goes wrong...

As development continues, it becomes increasingly important that we understand the distinction between humans and artificial intelligence to find ways for them to coexist.

4. **Machine Learning: The Quick and Dirty** - Machine learning is vital to AI, transforming our relationship with technology. The tech behind it lets systems learn, find patterns in data, and make choices without us. It's similar to how humans learn from experience, but on an extensive and fast scale, our brains can't even comprehend it.

Here's how it works... First, the program learns from a dataset by following an algorithm. Then, it analyzes the data to discover patterns between all the pieces of info inside it. Finally, this knowledge predicts outcomes or makes informed decisions about unseen data. In easy terms, we're teaching a machine to have human-like understanding and thinking.

Spotify uses machine learning for its music recommendations. It knows exactly what songs you love and hate based on which you play the most, skip, or look up frequently. This info alone makes its suggestions more personalized than other platforms, making it harder for you to resist listening to that new hot artist your friend mentioned.

Although machine learning seems like an advanced way to build a song playlist at first glance, its impact also expands into many vital areas. One example is banking fraud detection, where algorithms help identify odd patterns inside transactions that could indicate fishy activity. They can point out any similarities in real-time by comparing new transactions with historical data.

But beyond excellent playlists and safe banks, machine learning's power lies in its versatility. Similar algorithms are used in healthcare, where doctors can diagnose diseases faster and recommend treatments better thanks to these systems' predictions. Self-driving cars also utilize it to process massive amounts of incoming information from sensors and make accurate driving choices in split seconds.

As we develop this type of AI, one thing becomes clear: there isn't much it can't do. Thanks to machines being able to learn like humans, we're inching closer to a world of intuitive technology explicitly made for us and our problems.

5. **Deep Learning, Deeper Confusions** - Deep learning is a specialized branch of machine learning. It's fascinating in its own right and distinguished by a distinct feature – the use of neural networks with multiple layers. By working through these layers, deep learning models can analyze and interpret different aspects of data. In essence, it functions similarly to how our human brains process information.

Each layer processes unique details from the input and passes it on to the next layer. This complex structure allows for flexibility in interpreting unstructured data and enables us to handle large amounts of it. In contrast, traditional machine learning models cannot make sense of unstructured data sets.

This unparalleled capacity makes deep learning models particularly effective at handling images and speech. For example, whenever you unlock your phone with your face or command assistants like Siri or Alexa, there's some form of deep learning behind the scenes.

As you may know, Apple's Face ID system uses deep learning algorithms to recognize facial patterns with thousands of data points. Similarly, virtual assistants learn how we speak and identify different users' voices using deep learning techniques.

If you've ever been inside a Tesla vehicle, you've witnessed another instance of deep learning. The car's built-in technology processes data from various sensors to understand its environment better than most humans could imagine doing – all while driving! These cars collect massive amounts of data, which they use to adapt their speed, direction, and other safety precautions accordingly.

I could list examples all day, but you get the picture by now. Deep learning doesn't just push our technological limits; it brings us closer to a world where machines can "understand" things as we do. With advancements like this happening before our eyes every day, we should be excited about what the future holds.

6. **Neural Networks: Brainy Bots -** Neural networks are a marvel of modern technology. They take the structure and function of the human brain and create an interconnected system of neurons that process and transmit information. As our neurons do, each node in a neural network processes its piece of the puzzle, forming an understanding or decision. This means neural networks can adapt to changing inputs - something human brains excel at.

The adaptability and sophistication of neural networks make them highly effective for image and speech recognition tasks. For example, voice-activated assistants use these networks to understand what people say and discern words' meanings even in noisy environments or when accents are present. In image recognition, neural networks analyze images to identify objects and faces accurately.

A compelling application of neural networks is in handwriting recognition. The technology that converts handwritten text into digital form has made it possible to process and store handwritten documents electronically. It's a beautiful marriage between old-fashioned pen-and-paper writing and today's digital world.

In medicine, particularly in diagnosis, neural networks have been put to taking medical imaging like MRI scans or pathology slides and identifying patterns that point towards diseases like cancer. For example, these networks have been trained in pathology to recognize cancerous cells within tissue samples. And this power is not about technical efficiency; it's about saving lives by interpreting subtle patterns in medical data that humans could easily miss.

This line of work has led experts to believe these networks will become more integrated into healthcare as they evolve. Not only can they help us diagnose diseases, but they also hold the potential for gaining new insights into treatment methods.

Looking further into the future, where their capabilities have grown even more than what we can imagine now, we could see these systems being utilized in fields beyond our imagination. With every step forward in AI technology, the gap between human intelligence and machine processing power gets shorter and shorter.

7. **Algorithms: The Secret Sauce** - Algorithms are the heart of AI. They're the guiding structure by which an AI makes decisions and functions. These algorithms use rules or instructions to process data, which is utilized to drive decisions. There is a wide range of these algorithms that all serve different purposes. On one end, simple linear algorithms do straightforward tasks, like following steps in a recipe. On the other end, complex adaptive algorithms are used in machine learning. These things learn and adapt based on new data they get and are as powerful as they are versatile.

Just look at Google's search algorithms. They go through billions of web pages in a vast online world to find exactly what you want. Not only do they rank based on relevance, but they also rank sources by authority. All of this happens in a fraction of a second, too! It's like having an incredibly efficient librarian who can instantly find what book you need from a library that spans the entire world.

In finance, algorithmic trading shows us just how fast AI can be in a different light than search engines. Complex AI algorithms trade stocks at volumes and speeds that no human could ever do. These super-fast robots analyze market data, predict trends, and make trading decisions, all within milliseconds. Not only that, but they're constantly learning from patterns found in markets themselves! The more experienced they get with needs, the more accurate and sophisticated they become. This helps with the efficiency of financial markets and brings forth new strategies to try out when trading.

These algorithms' power comes from their ability to process vast amounts of data, identify patterns, make quick decisions with them accurately, and reshape many industries around us today.

They're quite something, aren't they?

8. **Data: AI's Food** - Data is the foundation supporting AI's pillars. Data quality, quantity, and variety determine how well AI can function. Think of it as fuel for a car: the better the energy you put in, the better your vehicle performs. The same goes for AI — high-quality, diverse, and vast amounts of data enable machine learning systems to learn more effectively, give more accurate predictions, and produce more reliable outcomes.

Let's take weather models as an example. We've seen remarkable improvements in their accuracy over time. A significant reason for these improvements is the availability of extensive data sets from different sources like satellites and sensors. These sources provide vast information on atmospheric conditions, temperature, humidity, etc. Machine learning models ingest this data and learn from past patterns to current conditions, making increasingly accurate predictions about the weather. It's a dance between algorithms and data that helps us plan our days, protect ourselves from extreme weather events, and understand climate change better.

The power of data also shines in language translation services such as Google Translate. These services rely on vast amounts of linguistic data to train their models. This data comes from different sources, such as books, websites, and real-time translations. They're pivotal because they make translation possible at a contextual level.

When new languages are added to these systems, they undergo training, where they learn to understand that language based on its characteristics — all by sifting through the available data.

It's almost magical how this ocean of information can be turned into actionable insights by AI so that we can benefit from them. In each application scenario—whether predicting weather or translating languages—AI uses algorithms to find patterns in our data that would otherwise be impossible for humans alone.

As we continue to generate more data daily, AI will only keep improving at using it. With that, we will discover further possibilities to apply AI across various fields such as healthcare, education, business, and entertainment.

9. **Supervised vs. Unsupervised Learning -** In AI, two methods mimic different learning styles — supervised and unsupervised.

Supervised learning is like having a teacher stand beside students as they learn. In this method, an AI model is trained on a labeled dataset where each piece of data comes with the correct answer. So, it's like giving the model a set of questions and their answers and telling it to learn to associate one with the other. This method is particularly effective in applications where we know what we're looking for and can identify it when we find it. For example, email spam filters are trained with pre-labeled emails as 'spam' or 'not spam.' The model learns from these labels and starts identifying patterns and characteristics of spam over time, eventually improving its ability to filter out unwanted emails.

On the other hand, unsupervised learning is like letting a student explore a subject independently without instructions. Here, an AI model is trained on unlabeled data — meaning its task is to find structure in chaos without knowing what that structure should look like. This method excels in scenarios where we don't understand what we're looking for or don't have predefined categories set up. A great example of this would be customer segmentation in marketing. In this application, unsupervised learning algorithms will analyze customer data and identify distinct groups or segments within the customer base based on shared characteristics found in the data, such as purchasing behavior or preferences. These segments are precious for targeted marketing and personalized customer experiences.

Supervised and unsupervised learning have unique advantages and are suitable for different problems. Supervised learning shines when the goal is transparent, so it can learn quickly and make predictions easily based on new data inputs. On the flip side, unsupervised learning has an edge over supervised learning when uncovering hidden patterns and structures in data that we might not know exist.

These methods drive many AI applications and highlight how versatile AI's learning capabilities can be. Whether following a set path or forging a new one, this tech is up to the task — no matter how complex or seemingly mundane.

10. Reinforcement Learning: Trial and Error - Reinforcement learning is a fascinating branch of machine learning. It's similar to trial-and-error learning in humans and animals. AI systems learn by doing, interacting with their environment, making decisions, and understanding the consequences. The process involves rewards and penalties that encourage the AI system to make decisions that produce positive outcomes.

Think of an AI system like a kid on a playground learning to do things right. Every little move it makes can result in a reward or penalty, so it quickly learns from those outcomes. This feedback loop encourages the AI system to repeat actions that lead to rewards and avoid those actions that result in penalties.

For example, if an AI robot is trying to pick up something, it must keep pushing until it gets it right multiple times. I taught it what not to do each time until it finally got it right. So, the robot gets better at picking up objects over time and with more tries. It fine-tunes its movements and decision-making process as time goes on.

Another good example is gaming; look at DeepMind's AlphaStar program, which mastered strategy games like StarCraft II. In this game, the AI competes against human players and learns from each loss or win. It knows it can't make the same moves as before because the players are likely expecting it now.

Reinforcement learning opens up new possibilities for AI development because the system can now learn from its experiences instead of just getting answers from data. And while there's still so much room for growth and improvement within this specific learning method, things look very bright for reinforcement learning.

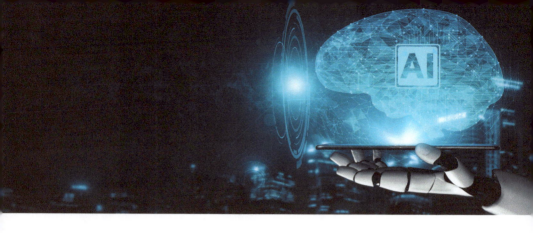

CHAPTER 2
AI FOR THE COMPLETE BEGINNER

Chapter 2, "AI for the Complete Beginner," is like an AI kindergarten but without nap time and with more algorithms. It's designed for those who think AI is still about Spielberg movies and robots taking over the world. Here, we gently hold your hand (digitally, of course) and guide you through the ABCs of AI, ensuring you don't get lost in the technical jungle.

We start with "AI Myths Debunked," where we separate AI fact from Hollywood fiction. Think of it as the myth-busting section where we reassure you that AI isn't going to turn your toaster into a plotting super-villain. This part clears up common misconceptions and sets the record straight so you can navigate the AI world without unnecessarily fearing a robot apocalypse.

Next, we dive into "Simple AI Experiments at Home." This is where AI gets personal and hands-on. You'll learn about easy experiments you can try at home, like training a basic chatbot or using AI to sort your digital photo collection. It's like a DIY project, but instead of ending up with a wonky bookshelf, you get a relaxed AI experience.

"Understanding AI News" is for those scratching their heads at tech headlines. We help you decode the newspeak of AI, turning those cryptic articles into understandable stories. It's like having a tech-savvy friend explain the news over coffee.

In "Basic AI Concepts Explained," we break down complex AI ideas into bite-sized, easy-to-digest morsels of knowledge. No heavy jargon, no bewildering concepts – just clear, straightforward explanations. It's like learning to cook a gourmet meal with AI concepts instead of exotic ingredients.

"AI and Your Privacy" addresses the elephant in the digital room – how AI interacts with your data. This section is like a guide to keeping your digital house locked, ensuring AI doesn't become an uninvited guest in your private life.

"The Human Side of AI" reminds us that behind every AI algorithm, there's a human story. This part explores how AI impacts real people, from job changes to lifestyle shifts. It's about understanding that AI isn't just a tech phenomenon; it's a human one, too.

"AI in Everyday Language" is where we translate AI-speak into plain English. It's like an AI Rosetta Stone, helping you understand AI terms and concepts without needing a tech dictionary.

"The Limitations of AI" brings a dose of reality, showing that AI, like humans, has its flaws and limitations. It's a reminder that AI isn't all-knowing and all-powerful, and sometimes, it still needs a little help from its human friends.

"Preparing for an AI-Driven Future" is like a training montage for the upcoming AI era. It's about gearing up for a world where AI is more common, ensuring you're ready and equipped to face the future.

"AI and Creativity: Can Machines Be Creative?" explores the intriguing intersection of AI and art. Can AI write a hit song? Paint a masterpiece? This section looks at the creative side of AI, which might not be Picasso yet but is trying its best.

"AI for the Complete Beginner" is your friendly guide through the world of AI, perfect for those just starting their journey. It's like AI 101, taught in a fun, engaging way – no tech degree required. So, come on in, the AI water's fine, and by the end of this chapter, you'll be swimming with the digital dolphins.

11. **AI Myths Debunked -** For AI beginners, separating facts from fiction is essential. We live in an era where AI is as much a myth as it is hype. A common belief is that AI can think and feel like humans. As of right now, this isn't true at all. AI doesn't have consciousness or emotions. It doesn't even have feelings, let alone the ability to think and feel like we do. That's a human thing. It's just a tool, albeit incredibly advanced, created and controlled by humans. It performs particular tasks efficiently, such as data analysis, pattern recognition, or automating repetitive tasks — without the human experience of consciousness or emotions.

Another myth people believe when it comes to AI is the fear that AI will eventually surpass human intelligence and put us in the science fiction scenarios we see in movies. Reality check: It's nowhere near close to having general intelligence or versatile thinking like we humans have in our heads. The advancements made so far are remarkable but direct those thoughts towards how they're focused on specific tasks rather than anything else beyond their narrow work range. General AI is just theoretical at this point.

AI job loss is something else that tends to put people in a frenzy to make them scared of what kind of future we're walking into with this stuff around us all day long, too. I mean, who can blame them? In reality, it won't be the end of jobs as we know them once these things gradually start taking over the workplace. Technological advancements alone have always shaped history with their fun little disruptions everywhere and anywhere possible. While yes, AI will automate specific tasks, such as dangerous ones or those being repeated on a loop all day, every day — this always opens doors for other opportunities elsewhere for different people, sparking new industries! So, nothing is ever really lost in technology and AI.

It's safe to say that AI beginners need to understand what it is, but most importantly, what it isn't. Both its potential and limitations should be appreciated. With things as advanced as AI, you have to approach it with a super clear understanding of everything it can and can't do with the ethical aspect of its deployment, too. Striking that balance will allow us to use this kind of technology responsibly and effectively to shape our future into one where AI complements our human capabilities for the greater good.

12. **Simple AI Experiments at Home -** It's a great way to learn and make sense of this often-intimidating technology. Starting with AI can be overwhelming because of its complexity and the jargon that often surrounds it. But breaking it down through practical, hands-on experiences can help give you a better idea of what AI is about.

If you're starting from scratch, plenty of introductory programming courses online can help you on your journey. Most of these courses now have AI modules tailored for beginners, introducing you to the basics and gradually diving deeper into more specific AI topics. These courses are perfect for those who don't have any prior experience in the field.

And if you get intimidated by coding, don't worry. Tools like Google's Teachable Machine can also help get you started. The teachable machine allows people to create simple machine-learning models without coding anything. It's an easy-to-use platform where you train the system to recognize images, sounds, or poses using a graphical interface. Tools like this make AI more approachable and demonstrate its potential in a fun and interactive way.

Experimenting with a Chatbot interaction can be fun. This experiment explores AI's ability to process and respond to natural language. You'll need a computer or smartphone with internet access to interact with various online AI chatbots, such as OpenAI's ChatGPT, Google's Dialogflow, or Replika. Engage these bots in conversations by asking multiple questions, from general knowledge queries to personal advice or humor. Observe how each bot responds to the same questions, paying attention to their relevance, coherence, and creativity. The goal is to compare the responses and determine which bot appears the most human-like, shedding light on their language understanding and generation capabilities.

These first-hand experiences will be invaluable for understanding AI concepts because you'll see how they work and how they're trained. This practical approach also demystifies AI and shows its usefulness when solving real-world problems.

It also sparks curiosity! Once you understand the basics, I guarantee you'll want to know more and explore further. Whether that means taking more advanced courses or participating in online communities — there's always room for growth in this field.

The first step is jumping in with beginner-friendly tools like these courses and platforms. They show that AI isn't just for experts but accessible to everyone willing to learn!

13. **Understanding AI News** - Understanding and critically assessing AI news. AI seems to be in every headline in our current age, but not everything is as groundbreaking as it appears. With it being a hot topic right now, I'm sure you've noticed some things are more hyped than they should be. This messes up any perception of AI progress and capabilities for beginners. It's essential to seek information from reputable sources when starting because their balanced and well-researched information will give you a realistic understanding of the world of AI.

One thing everyone can do is stop clicking on sensationalized headlines. Media outlets do this all the time to draw readers. These headlines usually oversimplify or exaggerate an article, so pay no mind to them because if something sounds too good to be true, it probably is.

It's also helpful to learn how to differentiate between different types of AI and their applications. Just like there are so many ways cars can be made, there are many kinds of AI with their specific uses. Essential automation tools for complex machine learning algorithms fall under the "AI" umbrella. By knowing these basics, you can accurately judge how significant new developments and breakthroughs are.

This knowledge isn't only helpful for understanding current AI tech but also its future possibilities. It allows you to step back and appreciate legitimate advancements while acknowledging any limitations and challenges in the field. Remember that we live in a world where technology constantly evolves, so staying informed and critical is vital if you want to keep up with its rapid pace.

14. **Basic AI Concepts Explained** - It's critical to grasp the basics of AI, particularly if you're starting in a vast field. Differentiating between AI, machine learning, and deep learning sets the stage for future exploration. Understanding these differences will place you on a sturdy platform for further education.

AI, or Artificial Intelligence, is indeed the most general term of the three. It refers to machines and systems that can complete tasks that require human intelligence. This covers many capabilities, such as understanding language and recognizing objects. The concept of AI is overarching; it encompasses every way we can make machines mimic or replicate our intelligence and behavior.

Machine learning is where we start specializing in things. In this subset of AI, machines are made to learn from data without being explicitly programmed for specific tasks. Unlike traditional programming, where you'd have to write code for every action and decision the computer will make, machine learning will look at data examples (the set it was given) and learn how to process those examples into rules.

Next up is deep learning — another specialization in machine learning. Deep Learning involves many layers of neural networks (hence "deep"). These multi-layered neural networks can process and interpret vast amounts of complex data. This method excels at tasks like image and speech recognition, where complexity and volume are too much for more straightforward machine learning techniques. Because deep learning models have so many interconnected layers, they can identify patterns quicker than other models.

For beginners, understanding these differences isn't just about knowing what all three terms mean… It's about appreciating how sophisticated AI is, what it's capable of doing right now, and what it can do in the future as we continue making advancements at each level. These basic concepts become building blocks that'll allow you to understand more advanced concepts as you dive deeper into AI's rabbit hole. So, it's a great starting point for anyone interested in the field.

15. **AI and Your Privacy** - Privacy with AI is a growing concern. Nowadays, AI is so intertwined with our daily lives that the amount of information collected and processed is enormous. Usually, this includes personal info, like our search habits and what we've bought. Then, it goes as far as where we go and even our biometric data. So, understanding how all this data gets collected, used, and protected isn't just for people interested in AI, but it's for everyone in the digital age.

Beginners or anyone using today's technology should know device and application privacy settings. Through these settings, you can usually control what gets collected and utilized from you. The average person probably doesn't understand how much information they're giving away about themselves, so looking through those settings can be eye-opening. Plus, it'll help keep your data safe.

Globally, various laws have been established to safeguard data, and everyone needs to be aware of them. A prime example is the General Data Protection Regulation (GDPR) in the European Union, designed to empower individuals with greater authority over their data. Understanding your entitlements under such regulations is beneficial, particularly when deciding where and how to disclose your information. These laws typically mandate that companies disclose the nature and purpose of the data they collect and provide individuals with options to access or request the deletion of their information.

A lot more is going to come up regarding AI and privacy. As AI systems get more complex and widespread, the challenge of balancing its benefits with protecting individual privacy grows increasingly important. This isn't just something technical but societal, with questions about ethics, trust, and what kind of future we want.

For anyone new to AI, understanding these privacy considerations is part of becoming an informed technology user. It's all about knowing potential risks and protecting your info early. Since AI will only keep growing, staying informed and vigilant about privacy will always be crucial to navigating the digital world.

16. The Human Side of AI - You hit the nail on the head: AI is as much about people as technology. The human element is just as, if not more important than, the algorithms and data. Everyone involved can make or break AI, from the developers and researchers to the end-users.

And you have to consider how AI affects people. There are a lot of ethical implications brought by this technology. Think privacy, employment, or even social dynamics.

Another big one is biases in AI systems. Data dictates how well an algorithm performs. And if that data has a bias, so will the predictions and decisions made by that algorithm. That's why biases can be a big problem in criminal justice or hiring practices using AI.

Building ethical AI ensures that these technologies benefit society overall. It means having efficient and effective systems while being fair, transparent, and accountable for everything they do.

For end-users (which usually means all of us), we need to understand how AI shapes our world. This way, everyone can make informed decisions about how they use it.

The human aspect of AI development is just as important as the technical part of it. It needs to consider values and rights to be effective when utilized by anyone who makes it a part of their lives — which includes all of us nowadays.

17. **AI in Everyday Language** - It doesn't have to be intimidating. Explaining AI in everyday language can make it much more digestible, especially for beginners just starting.

For example, your smartphone's camera has AI built into it. Instead of getting caught up in the algorithms and neural networks that make it work, you could describe it as a tool that makes your pictures look better without needing to be a pro. It's like having a virtual assistant working right on your camera, adjusting the settings based on your location. If you're in a dim place, it knows to brighten things up so you can get that perfect shot. Out and about with all types of sunlight? It'll find the ideal balance between not overexposing and keeping your picture clear.

This explanation is relatable because everyone wants to take good pictures, but not everyone can be considered a photographer. We can all appreciate just how convenient this is!

By breaking down complex concepts into things we do every day, we make learning them feel like second nature. Just think about when someone explains something to you, and they make it sound so straightforward after the fact. That's the feeling we want people new to exploring AI to have because once they understand how it can simplify daily tasks, they'll desire to learn more about what else they can use it for!

18. **The Limitations of AI** - One of the most essential things about AI is understanding its limitations. We must remember that even though it's super impressive, it's not magic. It isn't a solution to all our problems; AI can only make decisions based on what it's programmed for and trained with. So, the system can predict and drive choices, but only within a fixed set of boundaries.

Another thing we should note is how reliant AI is on data. It needs lots of it to learn and improve over time. But depending on that data also means that the outcome wouldn't be any different if it were trained with biased or incomplete material. The ethical side of AI is affected by this because it means mistakes will be made if the system isn't fed diverse or representative datasets.

Recognizing all this lets us set realistic expectations for what we're given. Sure, AI's helpful, but it has its downsides too. Therefore, we can use them where they excel and find other solutions where they don't.

Lastly, recognizing these limitations also clarifies how important responsible AI development is. By knowing the extent of our tools, we can ensure they align with our values by using them transparently and ethically with accountability in mind.

19. **Preparing for an AI-Driven Future -** Being prepared for an AI-driven future is crucial. As AI becomes a regular part of our lives, equipping ourselves with the knowledge and skills needed to succeed in this rapidly changing landscape will only become more necessary.

One of the most significant parts of preparing is recognizing AI skills that can't be easily replicated. Critical thinking, creativity, and emotional intelligence are just a couple of examples. While AI can dominate jobs involving data analysis and pattern recognition, it always falls short when its end goal or genuine understanding of human emotions is required. So, making sure we're comfortable and able to use these skills effectively will put us at an advantage where we're left as second nature once AI becomes even more common than it already is.

Another way to stay ahead of the curve is by keeping up with the constant changes in development, which help us understand how they'll impact different industries. The field of AI is constantly evolving, so making sure we're aware of what's happening will assist us in making informed decisions about leveraging AI for our benefit.

Lastly, using AI as a tool rather than trying to replace our expertise with it will be vital in adapting to create a high-level balance between harnessing its potential and being uniquely skilled as humans. An example would be how AI-powered data analysis tools can assist professionals in making better decisions but also need human intervention to interpret and apply those insights effectively.

In short, getting ready for an AI-driven future means finding a balance between using it as much as possible and remembering our unique ways. We have strengths that machines don't have, so staying true to those while learning new ones will set us up perfectly for success in an AI-driven world.

20. **AI and Creativity: Can Machines Be Creative?** - AI - its creativity, or at least the ability to mimic creativity, can be exciting. Whether AI can be genuinely creative is a topic that has been debated for some time. However, Artificial Intelligence (AI) and the arts are still debated.

AI has shown time and time again how remarkable it is in creating art, music, and literature by learning from thousands of existing works. Sometimes, it can even develop pieces that can't be told apart from those created by humans. Based on AI's patterns and styles, collaborating with it is impressive. However, some argue that true creativity only comes from original thought and emotion... something AI doesn't have.

Most of our emotions come from personal experiences; thinking outside the box (a human trait) is where most ideas also come from. Sure, AI can recognize patterns, but it does not possess the human qualities that make true creativity possible.

Even though it might not have natural creativity like humans do, there's no denying AI's significant role in enhancing human creativity - acting like a creator assistant. It offers new ways to express ideas better than we ever could. Suppose artists and musicians are willing to open their minds to this technology. In that case, collaborate with AI systems to explore all sorts of novel styles, generate new ideas, or experiment with different forms of expression.

What would usually take days, if not weeks, for us to think up or even comprehend... takes only seconds for AI.

Sure, we might've figured out how far we can go with this technology, but who knows what doors it will open in the future? We're seeing these ideas become more common, so we'll have to wait and see what happens next. It's next - exciting stuff!

CHAPTER 3
AI IN YOUR DAILY LIFE

Welcome to Chapter 3, "AI in Your Daily Life," where we reveal how Artificial Intelligence (AI) has sneakily crept into our lives like a cat burglar, except it's stealing our chores and making life easier instead of nabbing the family silver. This chapter is like a detective story, uncovering the hidden AI in our everyday routines. It shows that AI isn't just for tech whizzes – it's for everyone, including your grandma, who just discovered emojis.

First, we explore the world of smartphones, where AI is the unseen genie in the device, granting wishes from "Find me the nearest coffee shop" to "Take a selfie that hides my bad hair day." We delve into how AI makes these pocket-sized wizards smarter, helping us navigate, communicate, and even take better photos (because who doesn't want to look good in a selfie?).

Then, we tiptoe into social media, where AI is the puppet master behind the scenes, deciding what we see in our feeds. It's like a personal DJ, but for content, ensuring that your cat videos are always queued up. This section examines how AI shapes our online experiences, sometimes making us wonder, "How did it know I wanted a sweater with cats on it?"

Streaming services follow, where AI takes on the role of a psychic, predicting what movie or TV show you'd like to watch next. It's like having a friend who knows your taste in movies so well that they deserve their own Oscar. We explore how AI's recommendations keep us glued to our screens, binge-watching shows we didn't even know we'd love.

In e-commerce, AI emerges as the ultimate personal shopper, suggesting products with uncanny accuracy. It's like having a shopping assistant who knows you better than you understand yourself and never judges your late-night impulse buys.

We then turn the lights on smart homes, where AI is the invisible butler, managing everything from your playlist to your thermostat. It's making homes so smart that they might start giving us life advice soon.

The chapter also takes a peek into healthcare, where AI is like a diagnostic ninja, helping doctors spot health issues with the precision of a seasoned surgeon. It's not just about fancy gadgets; it's about saving lives and making healthcare smarter.

In finance, AI turns into a number-crunching wizard, managing risks and your retirement fund because who wouldn't want a crystal ball for their finances?

Transportation is up next, where AI is the excellent chauffeur of self-driving cars, promising a future where we can say, "Look, Ma, no hands!" while commuting.

We wrap up AI in gaming and education, where it's transforming how we play and learn. AI is the teacher who never gets tired and the gaming buddy who's always up for a challenge.

"AI in Your Daily Life" reveals the AI hiding in plain sight, making our lives more convenient, entertaining, and connected. It's a chapter that says, "AI is here, and it's more down-to-earth than you thought." So, buckle up for a tour of your AI-infused daily life – no tech jargon, just fun facts and a newfound appreciation for the intelligent world around you.

21. **Smartphones: Your Pocket-Sized AI -** These gadgets we use daily have grown to become highly complex devices. What was once a tiny communication tool has developed into a pocket-sized AI hub that fits our pockets. It's wild how much they can do if you think about it. Virtual assistants like Siri and Google Assistant are personal aides who answer questions, schedule appointments, and even tell jokes to cheer us up. Then there are the camera functionalities, which aren't just all show but professional-level capabilities that make every picture we take perfect.

But it's not just about being flashy and cool. The AI within these devices is constantly learning about us to optimize battery life, manage app usage, and more. One of my favorite things about smartphones is how easy they make texting people. Predictive text and voice recognition used to be novelties, but now they're essential tools for everyone who operates a phone daily. It makes typing messages faster by understanding how we speak and adapting to it.

AI in phones is also a worker who doesn't complain or ask for anything in return. It works silently in the background while learning how we interact with our devices and where we use them most often. This allows our phones to personalize our experience by suggesting playlists at specific times of the day or even adjusting their functionality to match our daily routines. Smartphones are so much more than tools; they're companions that have grown alongside humans as we've developed technology throughout history.

22. Social Media: AI's Playground - Social media platforms, the digital town squares of our era, showcase how seamlessly AI has integrated into the fabric of our daily digital interactions. The role AI algorithms play on these platforms is fascinating to consider. Analyzing our activities - what we like, share, and search for - every move is a puzzle piece that helps AI understand our preferences. This allows our social media feeds to be shaped and molded to reflect our interests. It doesn't stop there either; each click or swipe also shapes the ads we see. Tailored ads that perfectly align with what we want or need often appear on our screens when we least expect it.

But personalization doesn't stop at curating content and ads. It plays a vital role in content moderation as well. Though you may not know it, sophisticated algorithms filter out inappropriate content to ensure our online experiences aren't tarnished by offensive or harmful posts. They work around the clock as if they were vigilant guards to maintain safety within the digital environment we interact with daily. An example of this would be Facebook's news feed algorithm, which acts more as a curator rather than a tool that tailors content based on individual user preferences, ensuring all we see is relevant and engaging. A different yet equally important approach can be noticed when looking at X (previously known as Twitter) use of AI. Their platform utilizes advanced algorithms to detect and manage abusive or spammy posts to create healthier digital conversation space. This isn't easy, considering new content is generated by the second.

It's safe to say these applications are more than just technical marvels; they're essential in ensuring a relevant, enjoyable, and secure user experience on social media platforms. They work tirelessly in the background, sifting through the overwhelming amount of data from every part of the world so that you can present content that aligns with your interests while keeping the toxic elements of the online world out of reach. These algorithms are our unsung heroes, making our online lives easier in ways we don't even realize. As the digital expansion continues, one thing is clear - AI will play a vital role in how we connect, share, and engage with each other online.

23.Streaming Services: The AI DJ - There's no denying that streaming services like Spotify and Netflix have revolutionized media consumption. It's all thanks to AI. Remember when we had to sift through channels or CDs to find something to watch or listen to? Now, these platforms have brought a new level of convenience and personalization to our fingertips.

Take Spotify, for example. It's not just a music streaming service; your personal DJ knows precisely what you want to hear. The AI algorithms behind Spotify are so advanced that they don't just look at what you've played; they analyze your listening habits, diving into the nuances of your musical tastes. This is how the Discover Weekly feature works – it's like a magical music cauldron that stirs up a playlist every week specifically tailored to your preferences, introducing you to new songs and artists perfectly aligned with whatever the heck it is you like!

And then there's Netflix. Remember when it was just a DVD rental service? It's a streaming giant whose success heavily depends on how well it uses AI to enhance our viewing experience. Netflix's recommendation engine is fantastic; it doesn't just consider what you've watched; it looks at when you observe, how often you pause or skip, and what genres you prefer — all this data helps Netflix suggest shows and movies that will likely captivate you. Whether it's a lazy Sunday afternoon or a late-night binge-watch session, Netflix always has the perfect suggestion.

The AI-powered personalization by streaming services has completely changed the game regarding discovering good content and enjoying it in ways we never thought possible. It took out all of the effort from us viewers and made content discovery effortless and fun — primarily fun because sometimes I feel like these platforms know us better than we understand ourselves. As a result, our experience with media consumption isn't really about consuming anymore but about exploring new things and discovering stuff guided by AI that understands our tastes and preferences. It's truly fascinating to be a part of, and I can't wait to see where it takes us next.

24. **E-commerce: AI, the Personal Shopper -** Artificial Intelligence (AI) has transformed the e-commerce landscape. You can now experience a future where shopping is more than just a task – instead, it's an experience catered for you. Online retailers are no longer just stores but personal shoppers who understand your needs better with every click.

The way AI analyzes your browsing habits, purchase history, and even your searches is nothing short of genius. It doesn't just collect data; it learns about you, figures out likes and dislikes, and sometimes even anticipates what you need before you realize it. This approach has subtly yet significantly enhanced the shopping experience.

It's like having a friend who knows everything about you, guiding you through rows of infinite products in an aisle, suggesting only those that interest you. Not only does this make shopping more enjoyable, but it also makes it incredibly efficient.

Amazon is an example of this with its recommendation engine. The way it offers items that seem to be precisely what you're looking for is mind-blowing, even if you haven't thought of them yet! It's like the engine reads your mind and suggests new products using previous purchases and viewed products. It's fascinating and a bit eerie how accurate it can be!

However, AI's role in e-commerce isn't limited to recommending products. It also extends into customer service– those chatbots that offer assistance. Yep, they're AI too! They instantly provide help, answer questions, and solve problems, making your shopping experience smoother.

And then there's inventory management – AI's ability to predict demand and optimize stock levels is not something to be taken lightly. Gone are the days when we worry if our favorite product will go out of stock or if retailers' overstocking will be an issue.

AI in e-commerce isn't just a technological advancement; it's a paradigm shift in how we shop and interact with online retailers. It's made shopping more personal, efficient, and enjoyable – and I think it's just the beginning. As AI continues to evolve, it's compelling to wonder how much more personalized and seamless our shopping experiences will be.

25. **Smart Homes: Living in the Future -** You know, the whole concept of smart homes does feel like we're living in what used to be a futuristic fantasy. What was once an idea plucked out of a sci-fi novel is now our reality. Thanks to AI, our homes are transformed into everything we've ever wanted them to be.

Take smart thermostats, for example, like the Nest. It's not just a device hanging on the wall; it's like a roommate that knows your routine. It figures out when you wake up and leave for work and when you prefer your home to be relaxed and comfortable. Adjusting your home's temperature based on these patterns makes you comfy and saves energy. It's like having your little assistant working tirelessly to ensure your house feels perfect.

And what about those bright lights? Remember when we used to stumble in the dark trying to find the light switch? Our homes can brighten up when we step in or match our mood by changing colors. These lights can learn your preferences, too, like dimming down during dinner for a cozy atmosphere or lighting up while you read.

Even security has advanced light years with intelligent cameras and systems. They don't just record footage like old-school security cameras do. They're fitted with AI that can tell if something suspicious is happening and will notify you immediately. So, if someone strange shows up at your door at 3 AM, these cameras will inform you immediately.

However, AI in smart homes does more than connect all our devices; it also makes us more efficient and saves energy! Imagine controlling every device in your house through one app on your phone! But that's not even the best part; that title goes to how all these devices work together effortlessly, making our lives easier without us doing anything! And let's not even mention how they help save the environment!

AI in smart homes is like having an invisible personal assistant working around the clock to ensure your home is as comfortable, secure, and efficient as possible. It's mind-boggling how far technology has come and exciting to think about what might arrive next. Sometimes, I lay awake at night fantasizing about a future where I can tell my house, "Lights out," and it just happens!

26.Healthcare: Dr. AI - The role of AI in healthcare is transformative. It's like a medical revolution: more precise, more personalized, and more proactive than ever before. Diagnosis, treatment, and patient care have all been improved by advancements brought about by AI.

Take medical imaging. AI algorithms can analyze images with such detail that it's as if there's a superhuman consultant in the room. This is especially important for early diagnosis of diseases like cancer — the algorithms see things that people don't, spotting signs of illness at its earliest stages.

AI-driven tools like Merative L.P. Health acts as doctors' digital assistants, offering insights from vast medical information databases. The wealth of data that doctors can access allows them to make better decisions about patient care. It's like having a library and a team of researchers at your fingertips.

And then there are wearable devices with AI — these aren't just fitness trackers; they're health guardians that monitor your well-being 24/7. The data they collect helps catch potential issues before they become serious problems. It's like having a personal health monitor implanted under your skin.

Don't forget about drug discovery and personalized medicine, either! This is where AI shines brightest: tailoring treatments to individual genetic profiles. There is no longer just a one-size-fits-all approach to therapy; now, it's what works best for you.

AI in healthcare is changing the industry on many levels – offering new ways to treat patients differently than ever. With further evolution, it'll only get better!

27. Finance: AI Counts Your Cash - AI is essential in finance. Just think about it: an ultra-intelligent and analytical brain at work can ensure everything goes smoothly and smartly in the often-confusing world of finance. AI's integration has gone beyond impressive; it's revolutionizing the industry.

We can start with risk management. It's one of the most critical financial tasks - and now AI is a crucial tool. By analyzing customer data and market trends, AI algorithms can provide valuable insights into investment strategies. And oh boy, are they fast - They can process massive amounts of data so quickly that it makes your eyes spin. Quickly analyzing and responding to market changes is very useful when automating trading. Think about this: It's like having a crystal ball that gives investors and traders an edge in the financial market.

Next is Fraud detection – a primary concern for all banks and their customers. AI comes here as a very disciplined watchdog, constantly tracking transaction patterns for anything that could be out of the ordinary or fraudulent. The way AI can pick up on tiny little things that could indicate fraud is terrific – This prevents financial losses while enhancing trust and security in banking systems.

But hold on! We're not done yet! One of my favorite applications of AI in finance is user-friendly personal finance apps. They function more like personal financial advisors you carry around and fit in your pocket than apps. With some extra help from AI, these apps offer advice on budgeting and saving customized with your spending habits and financial goals in mind, making it easier for everyday people to do financially well-planned activities such as budgeting and saving.

AI adoption isn't just a technological advancement — it's game-changing. With its powers, financial services become more efficient across the board - More secure, too... but perhaps the best part is how personalized everything becomes; from big banks to individual users, AI empowers everyone in the financial ecosystem. It makes it easier to manage money, create more informed investment decisions, and protect against risks - Just about everything you could want from a financial tool.

It's so fascinating to see how AI is reshaping finance - And now I can't wait to catch it continue evolving and improving our daily lives.

28. **Transportation: Self-Driving Cars and AI Pilots -** There's no other way to say it: the changes that AI is making in the transportation industry are revolutionary. We're talking science fiction-level stuff here. Just look at self-driving cars, for example, once a concept from a movie, now coming to life. They're on their way to changing how we think of personal and public transportation. The idea that our vehicles will be navigating traffic and making quick decisions on the road is just flat exciting.

And the skies are experiencing a transformation as well with AI in aviation. Autopilot systems, once simple flight tools, are now highly advanced. These bad boys have been built to handle complex tasks so air travel can become safer and more efficient. And they aren't slowing down either as these systems continue to integrate even more advanced features for pilots as they manage flights in various scenarios.

One of the striking examples of AI advancements in aviation is Cirrus Aircraft's "Safe Return" system. This system is a godsend for passengers whenever something goes wrong with the pilot during a flight. They only need to press a little Safe Return Autoland button, which takes over everything else. It doesn't only look at landing options for the plane but also analyzes data like fuel level, weather conditions, and terrain to make the best decision possible on where to bring everyone back safely. It's unique how fast this works once it starts taking control; It lowers flaps, deploys landing gear, controls speed, and then gently touches down until all passengers get out.

These advancements aren't just made so we can show off technology; they're created to increase safety and efficiency naturally. The future of transportation looks nothing short of incredible thanks to these advancements in AI we've made already when on land or while flying above clouds. So, let's enjoy this time as we see and be a part of the revolution brought on by AI.

29. Gaming: AI's Playground, Part II - How the gaming industry has embraced AI is a testament to how technology can elevate art and entertainment to new heights. It's incredible to think that we've come this far. Now, AI isn't just used for non-player characters but for almost every aspect of the experience. This makes it more immersive, more challenging, and more personal than ever before.

Let's start with game development itself. Game developers have been given an extra set of hands. And not just any hands, brilliant ones that can bring incredibly complicated worlds to life. Procedural content generation is one example of this, where AI algorithms create huge, unique landscapes that are both detailed and challenging. This makes games intriguing and extends their replayability.

AI also analyses player behavior, which takes the fun personalization to a new level. Games can now understand how you play, adapt to your skill level, and anticipate what you like. Not only does this make sure you're always having a blast, but it keeps the game accessible, too.

'The Last of Us Part II' is an excellent example of what I'm talking about here — realistic, unpredictable enemy behaviors that add depth and challenge to the gaming experience. The enemies in these games no longer follow a set pattern; they think, react, and adapt, making each encounter unique and thrilling.

Not only is AI used in gaming technology, but it's also changing paradigms of how we experience them digitally. Instead of static, predictable environments, we move into dynamic living ecosystems that respond and adapt to our actions like real life.

And as AI grows, I can't help but be excited about what's to come with gaming. Realistic worlds? Smarter opponents? Experiences explicitly tailored for me? Count me in!

30. **Education: AI as the Personal Tutor -** AI's impact on education is mind-blowing. We're entering a time when learning will no longer be a one-size-fits-all situation. This technology will change the way we deliver and experience education. We are making it more tailored to our individual needs and lifestyles than ever before.

Let's take a second to think about AI-driven educational platforms. These aren't your average digital textbooks. They're personal tutors that can change based on how you learn and at what pace. The AI can adjust the course content accordingly if you best learn visually, interactively, or through detailed explanations. It's like having a custom-made learning experience to ensure each student can learn most comfortably. This approach is constructive for students who've struggled with traditional teaching methods.

Take Duolingo as an example here. Language learning used to scare people off, but AI makes it much more approachable now! Duolingo's AI algorithms help create a practical yet enjoyable learning path using interactive exercises and games to reinforce learning. It's like having a fun language coach by your side 24/7.

AI doesn't only benefit students, though; educators profit from it, too! Administrative tasks like grading assignments and providing feedback have been made much more straightforward than before, saving teachers the time they can spend on what they love: teaching, mentoring, and inspiring their students.

Our use of AI in education stretches even further, though. It breaks down the barriers to entrance to education by democratizing access throughout all levels of society. Everyone benefits from this tailored approach regardless of their backgrounds or abilities. I can't wait for what this technology has in store for us next!

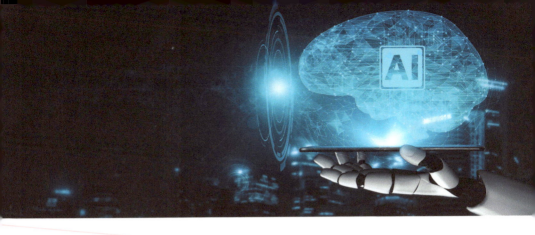

CHAPTER 4
AI AT WORK

In Chapter 4, "AI at Work," we roll up our sleeves and dive into the bustling world of Artificial Intelligence (AI) in the workplace. Think of this chapter as your all-access pass to the behind-the-scenes action where AI is the new intern, manager, and coffee machine repair person, all rolled into one. It's where we explore how AI is not just a fancy gadget in the boardroom but a hardworking team member reshaping industries from the ground up.

First, we peek into the business world, where AI is the new whiz kid on the block, crunching numbers and analyzing data faster than you can say "spreadsheet." We see how AI is helping businesses make decisions that are not just smart but Sherlock-Holmes-level smart. It's like having a crystal ball with algorithms and data instead of magic.

Then, we put on our hard hats and explore AI in manufacturing. AI is the super-efficient assembly line worker who doesn't take coffee breaks. We delve into how AI makes production lines faster and more intelligent, predicting maintenance issues before they become the reason for a bad day at work.

In agriculture, AI dons the hat of a high-tech farmer. It's out in the fields, ensuring healthy crops, predicting the weather, and probably scaring away the crows. This section shows how AI is helping farmers grow more food while using fewer resources, which is like having your cake and eating it, too.

The chapter also strolls through the corridors of marketing departments, where AI is the new creative genius, personalizing ads and content. It's like having Don Draper from "Mad Men," but in code form and without the vintage suits.

In customer service, AI steps in as the ever-helpful assistant, handling queries with the patience of a saint. We explore how AI chatbots revolutionize customer interactions, tirelessly answering questions at all hours and never asking for a day off.

We also peek into the HR department, where AI is helping hire and retain talent. It's like a matchmaker for jobs, ensuring the right people find the right roles, minus the awkward first dates.

Project management gets a tech makeover with AI, too. Here, AI is the ultra-organized project manager who never forgets a deadline and can predict problems before they happen. It's like having a crystal ball, but for Gantt charts.

AI is the digital superhero in cybersecurity, guarding against cyber threats and wearing a virtual cape. This section shows how AI is protecting valuable data from the villains of the digital world.

The chapter also sheds light on AI in research and content creation, where it's the innovative scientist and the creative artist, often at the same time.

"AI at Work" of "Bots & Brilliance" shows AI rolling up its virtual sleeves and getting to business. It's a chapter informing you that while

AI might be taking over some jobs, it's still far from mastering the office coffee blend. So, sit back, relax, and enjoy discovering how AI at work is more than just robots and algorithms – it's about more innovative, efficient, and, dare we say, more exciting ways of getting the job done.

31. **AI in Business: Beyond Spreadsheets** - The role of AI in revolutionizing businesses is genuinely remarkable. We might even be witnessing a significant shift in how companies operate. AI has proven to be more than just a tool; now, it's also a fundamental part of modern business practices. It can improve everything from daily operations to long-term strategies.

One of the significant ways that AI has impacted the business world is by automating tasks that are done all the time. This makes for the perfect assistant since they can tirelessly handle repetitive or time-consuming work. Human employees then use their brains on more complex and creative tasks. With this, not only will productivity increase, but so will opportunities for innovation and growth.

But let's not forget about predictive analytics because AI is good at this. When analyzing patterns and trends in large amounts of data, businesses can anticipate market shifts and understand customer needs before they're even there. Ultimately, this allows them to make informed decisions, giving them a unique competitive advantage. Staying ahead of the curve has never been easier.

In Customer Relationship Management (CRM), AI plays just as big of a role. Businesses used to believe that CRM systems were enough to manage customer data, but we've come a long way from then, thanks to tools like Salesforce's Einstein. What separates this tool from others is that instead of just managing customer data, it also uses AI to analyze it. When you combine these things, you'll receive personalized interactions and tailored services, resulting in one happy customer after another.

It doesn't end there; AI has also made its way into supply chain management, just like Amazon uses it with its warehouse robots and supply chain optimization. Tools like this help predict demand, optimize inventory, and ensure the supply chain runs smoothly. Traditional methods can't compare when it comes to precision and efficiency.

Simply put, AI isn't here to make businesses more efficient but to transform them. It does this by changing how businesses interact with customers and plan for the future. The possibilities of what it can do are endless, and we should be excited about it. As AI continues to evolve, there's no denying that it will play a much more significant role in driving business success in the future. It's a fantastic time to be a part of all this.

32. **AI in Manufacturing: Robots with a Cause -** The AI boom in manufacturing is mind-boggling. These days, the boundaries between science fiction and the natural world are more blurred than ever. Take, for example, intelligent factories; they were once far-off dreams, but now they're part of reality — changing how things are made.

Think about those robots powered by AI and sensors that can be found all over factory floors. They're not just machines; they're high-tech conductors with only one goal: to make the manufacturing process more efficient. Not only do these robots do jobs that we can't do because they're too repetitive or dangerous, but they also play an essential role in reducing downtime and improving safety — making factories safer and more reliable places to work.

And that's not even half of it — AI has a place in quality control, predictive maintenance, and product design. The accuracy of quality control has reached its peak with this tech. The human eye might miss out on flaws that AIs won't. This ensures that only perfect products make their way out of factories.

Predictive maintenance is another area where AI shines. It acts as if it's making accurate predictions with a crystal ball. By monitoring and analyzing machinery performance, AI can predict when a problem might pop up. This allows businesses to take action before costly issues come about. It's a proactive approach that minimizes cost and time while keeping production at full blast.

Lastly, we have product design. AIs can look at countless designs until they find the perfect one — which isn't something a human could accomplish in such a short time. Creating innovative products is essential, but ensuring mass production won't be an issue.

The bottom line here is simple: The integration of AI into manufacturing demonstrates our remarkable ingenuity. This integration turns what was once an inefficient industry into something efficient. The change isn't about being competitive anymore; it's about creating new possibilities and redefining what we know about manufacturing. The future of manufacturing is exciting with AI at the helm and all of its progress and innovation abilities. The possibilities are endless, and there's no doubt that the future holds nothing but opportunity for this industry.

33. **AI in Agriculture: High-Tech Farming -** Isn't it wild how AI brings an entirely new age of agriculture? Before our very eyes, farmers are taking this technology and implementing it into their work to make everything more efficient and effective. It's like a revolution in the field - literally! It's as if we're seeing a mix of long-standing practices with high-tech tech, changing everything about farming.

As I see it, AI in agriculture is like a superpower for farmers. Imagine looking at data from drones above you, satellites in the sky, and sensors rooted in the soil. This isn't just data collection — it's practically knowing every detail about your farm. That was unheard of only a few years ago. These tools help farmers make important decisions like planting, watering, and harvesting, leading them toward more efficient farming practices.

Thanks to AI-driven technologies, crops and soil have never had a better protector. They monitor things 24/7, including weather patterns and crop and soil health. Because of this, farmers can optimize agricultural practices for the highest yield possible. Instead of just letting the water soak into fields whenever they want, now they have the knowledge to know when each seed has its best shot at growing, with enough care for each plant as well. This crazy precision allows more productivity and promotes sustainable farming practices.

John Deere even uses AI and machine learning on their tractors and equipment… Their technology can adjust by itself depending on what kind of land it's on at any given moment right then and there! Imagine having an intelligent assistant collaborating with you, doing everything perfectly every time- whether tilling, planting, or harvesting. And nope — this isn't just making machinery smarter… It's pushing farmers to manage their land better, improving efficiency and crop yields.

AI in agriculture isn't just some advancement in technology… It completely changes the way we think about farming. We're going from a labor-intensive practice to using data and science. But this goes deeper than just improving yields. It's also about reducing environmental impact, securing food, and ensuring that farming will be sustainable for years. Thinking about the potential of AI in AG, it is incredible to imagine what it has in store for us.

34. **AI in Marketing: Selling Smarter** - AI's impact on marketing departments is staggering. It's just wild how much this technology is transforming everything. The field has become more precise, personalized, and responsive. Our ability to understand and engage with customers is at the next level. How we've even reached this point in the first place feels like a miracle.

Just look at the role AI algorithms play in analyzing consumer data. It used to be that we would spend hours crunching numbers to get an idea of what people might want. But now? It's like we're inside their heads! You can bet that if there's a trend or a preference that hasn't been capitalized on, AI will find it and allow us to build a strategy around it. This technology makes marketing campaigns extremely personalized and effective in ways we never thought possible before.

And then chatbots and virtual assistants? They're incredible, too! Always ready for some real-time personal customer service. These things are always available 24/7, and they don't sleep or take breaks- unlike you do anyway- which lets them answer questions, solve problems, and even recommend products without ever getting tired of doing so. Every interaction builds stronger bonds between brands and customers.

Now, let's talk about sentiment analysis quickly. Every AI-driven marketing team should always use this: knowing what people feel about your company's offerings and why they feel that way can make or break your brand so fast. I promise you won't see it coming.

You need to know how people feel about your stuff because you're already behind everyone else if you don't see what's trending. Being behind means being lost; when you're lost, you cannot make informed decisions about things like effective marketing strategies or branding changes to improve everything. It's not a good place to be.

Enough with all that; let me tell you what Coca-Cola is doing now. They're using AI-driven analytics to monitor their brand's reputation and the market. Social media and other sources constantly provide insights that allow them to see how people perceive their brand and whether it's trending. That's how they can stay ahead of the game and understand what strategies they should be working with.

So, in short, AI in marketing isn't just about speeding things up and making everyone more efficient -- although we try our best -- it's also about building a better connection with customers. Whether by tiny increments or huge bounds forward, it doesn't matter; the point is that we're always moving closer to our audience. The stronger the bond between them and brands, the more value both sides get from interacting.

I'm so incredibly excited for this tech's future growth! Seeing how it reshapes everything around us is unique. And if you love this field, then you should be too!

35.**AI in Customer Service: Chatbots and Beyond** - AI revolutionizes customer service. Getting help and support has become seamless thanks to this technological advancement. The introduction of chatbots and virtual assistants has provided 24/7 support, allowing customers to find solutions at any time.

Long queues are now a thing of the past. There's no more waiting on the phone or in chat windows. These bots can manage numerous queries all at once. They provide immediate responses and immediate resolutions. Not only does this reduce wait times, but it also increases the probability of instant problem-solving.

But how do these tools learn? And what can they do?

When the AI interacts with a customer, it isn't just collecting information for that singular transaction. They take that opportunity to learn, understand better, and improve themselves over time. This way, they become more effective in handling queries, even resolving issues before the customer asks.

Companies such as Zendesk and Freshdesk have integrated AI into their platforms. This significantly boosts company efficiency while also increasing customer satisfaction. Today's world is fast-paced and full of precious time — having a customer service system that is quick, responsive, and effective makes a massive difference in how customers perceive and interact with a brand.

AI doesn't just apply to direct customer interactions, though. It extends its influence to analyzing customer feedback as well as service calls. Doing so provides insights into common issues, allows companies to gauge consumers' sentiments, and identifies improvement areas. By understanding these patterns, businesses can make strategic changes to their products or services, leading to a better customer experience.

In short, automation isn't what AI's purpose is here; it's about creating a more responsive, efficient, and personalized user experience.

This innovation will forever change the future of how we interact with support systems.

36. **AI in HR: Hiring and Firing -** You betcha — no doubt, AI has a severe leg up on HR. It's like pouring gasoline on an already blazing fire: efficiency and objectivity have skyrocketed to levels we couldn't even dream of before. Talent acquisition and management is by far the most interesting.

Take the hiring process. Screening resumes was a tedious, often subjective task that took forever — not anymore, though. With AI, this process has been made much more efficient and fairer. Algorithms can quickly analyze resumes while picking relevant skills and experiences that match job requirements. This makes recruitment faster but also helps reduce biases—something we humans tend never to avoid. By focusing on data-driven evaluations, AI ensures candidates are selected based on their merits rather than subliminal preferences that might creep into human decision-making.

Oh, but wait, there's more! AI isn't just helping companies pick from the best of the best. It's also shaking things up by aiding in managing and retaining talent.

This is gold for companies, from pulling employee data like performance metrics and engagement levels to identifying patterns and predicting turnover. It lets them proactively address issues that may lead to employee dissatisfaction or attrition.

Is HR having a bad rep? It's not a problem when you know what employees always think! Just kidding...kind of.

I mean here that once these patterns are understood, HR can implement strategies to improve employee engagement and retention. Thus creating a better work environment for everyone involved.

But enough with all the talk! Let me give you an example of how IBM's Watson Career Coach uses AI to support employees' career development: it's like having a personal career advisor who will be honest with you every step of the way! But instead of an actual person, it's powered by AI, which provides personalized advice and job recommendations based on skills, experience, and aspirations.

So, AI in Human Resources isn't just about automating tasks. It's much more than that. It's a complete overhaul of HR practices — from hiring to talent management. By making HR practices more data-driven, fair, and focused on employee well-being, we can turn them into what they were always meant to be: efficient, equitable, and employee-centric.

I can't wait to see how AI continues to evolve and mold the future of HR. It won't stop here either; as you know, this is only getting started!

37. AI in Project Management: The Unbiased Overseer - Thanks to AI, we're in a new era of planning, executing, and managing projects. Just think about the efficiency and enhancement AI brings regarding decision-making in this field.

Let's take the ability of AI tools to predict project risks, for example. This could help you with having a foresight superpower when it comes to managing projects. By analyzing historical data and current project metrics, AI can identify potential hurdles or challenges that may pop up on your plate before they even become problematic. This skill to predict is invaluable as it allows project managers to get ahead of issues and strategize how to mitigate risks for smoother execution.

Next, look at resource allocation. AI's ability to suggest optimal resource allocation is significant. It can analyze various factors, such as team members' skills, resource availability, and project timelines, to recommend the most efficient use of resources. It doesn't only help in increasing productivity, but it also ensures that projects are completed within budget and on time.

Oh, did I mention that it also helps automate routine administrative tasks? These tasks, although necessary, can be very time-consuming and sometimes steal attention away from more critical areas of project management. With the automation process from AI, project managers will be able to focus more on essential components of the project rather than getting stuck with scheduling, reporting, and tracking processes.

Take Microsoft's Project Cortex, for example; organizing company data into knowledge networks helps make access quick and efficient, aiding PMs in making decisions faster as information is crucial at specific points during decision-making.

It's about working faster and smarter with AI in Project Management. To be more proactive, efficient, and effective in their roles is the goal that everyone is trying to achieve by integrating AI into their everyday activities. As technology continues improving and further integrating these tools, we're excited to see how it will continue redefining the field. The future of project management is more organized, efficient, and data-driven, all thanks to AI.

38. **AI in Cybersecurity: Digital Shield** - With threats advancing daily, having a virtual bouncer on guard is always valuable. The technology can analyze and make sense of network traffic in real-time, which is impressive. It processes much more information than any human could hope to and does it quickly and accurately.

The system excels at identifying anomalies, too, things that could put security at risk. Do you know how humans get a gut feeling about something? That's what this is like. It recognizes when something doesn't belong or seem right, and that helps it spot potential security breaches early on.

It also learns from past incidents, which is arguably more impressive than anything else it does. Every time something goes wrong, the AI knows what it was and how to avoid it in the future. So, with each new breach attempt or attack, the AI becomes even better at handling them.

Take Darktrace, for example. It uses machine learning rather than just scanning and acting like nothing happened. Instead, it notices cyber threats as soon as they occur and takes care of them before they become an issue. This is super important because every second counts in this field.

But AI isn't just an assistant in the field; it's necessary. As we become even more digital than we are now, defense mechanisms have to be, too. Otherwise, everything will collapse around us one day. As of now, though, I think we're OK because, with AI's ability to evolve continuously to stay ahead of cybercriminals, there's nothing AI can't do if we keep advancing our tech while keeping safety in mind.

39. **AI in Research: Accelerating Discovery -** AI's role in research is monumental. It acts as a catalyst for groundbreaking discoveries and innovations. Think of it as a digital genius that can sift through complexities and vast datasets that would overwhelm human researchers. Its impact across various fields, from healthcare to environmental science, is revolutionary.

AI's ability to analyze immense datasets opens new frontiers in drug discovery and treatment methods in healthcare. Imagine AI algorithms combing through global medical records, research papers, and clinical trials at speed and depth—impossible to match by humans. This allows identifying potential drug candidates faster, accelerating the pace at which new treatments reach patients. It's like a super-powered research assistant that not only speeds up the process but also brings a level of precision in pinpointing effective therapies.

When it comes to environmental research, AI's contribution is equally significant. Its role in modeling climate change scenarios is game-changing. With AI, scientists can analyze complex ecological data, predict future trends, and simulate various scenarios—critical in understanding and preparing for the impacts of climate change. Additionally, in conservation efforts, AI helps monitor wildlife and ecosystems, detects changes, and identifies threats, making conservation efforts more effective and timelier.

Google's DeepMind is a prime example of AI's transformative impact on research. Its contribution to protein folding research solved a problem that had baffled scientists for decades. This breakthrough isn't just academic; it has profound implications for understanding diseases and developing new treatments. It's like the missing piece humans couldn't find themselves—AI found for them, giving way to new medical treatments.

AI in research isn't just about processing power or data analysis; It's about pushing boundaries in knowledge and capability. Enabling us to leap into understanding with innovation we've never seen before just years ago. As it continues to evolve—and integrate into various fields—I'm excited to see where we'll end up next while unraveling old mysteries, too.

40. **AI in Content Creation: The Artistic Bot -** AI's foray into the creative world is a sight. It's fascinating how it goes from data and analytics to being an artist, writer, and composer. Just looking at it challenges our traditional understanding of creativity.

Think about written content generated entirely by AI algorithms. These algorithms go beyond just squeezing words together. They study vast amounts of text to analyze language nuances, styles, and expressions. It's like having digital scribes that can imitate human writing styles so well that it can get hard to differentiate what was written by a human or an AI tool. From articles to poetry, there seems to be no limit to what these tools can produce.

Then you have AI in art and music. The way they create visual and auditory art is borderline sorcery. Analyzing existing works' patterns, styles, and techniques lets them make unique pieces that strike chords within us — things we'd expect from human creations. Imagine a machine composing music or painting a picture with colors and notes that evoke emotions and thoughts.

Take OpenAI's GPT-4 Plus as an example and see for yourself the creative potential of AI. It can write articles, poetry, and even code! We're talking about an AI system with an advanced understanding of human language and creativity — something we usually think only humans possess.

Honestly, this has massive implications in the real world — it can assist human creativity and define new artistic styles… heck, who knows what else?

AI going full-on creative mode isn't just another technological advancement; it's a cultural shift, too. Creating things we never thought possible before in ways we could only dream of expanding the boundaries of creation— hand in hand with humans! I wonder how far this will go when left to evolve freely. Will there be new ways for humans to interact with AI? How many more things will we learn from it? It's all exciting, and I can't wait to see the future of creativity when it decides to merge with AI.

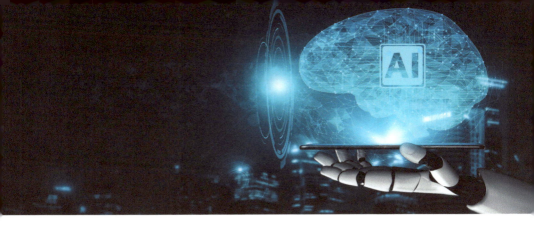

CHAPTER 5
AI FOR THE TECH ENTHUSIAST

In Chapter 5, "AI for the Tech Enthusiast," we roll out the red carpet for those who have a crush on technology, especially the kind that thinks for itself. This chapter is like a fan club meeting for AI enthusiasts, where we geek out over the cool, the quirky, and the downright mind-boggling aspects of AI. It's for those who prefer coffee with a dash of code and conversations sprinkled with tech jargon.

We kick things off with "Building Your AI Projects," essentially DIY for the digital age. Here, we dive into how you can create your own AI butler or a simple chatbot that laughs at your jokes. It's like arts and crafts, but we use algorithms and data sets instead of glitter and glue.

Next, we decode "Understanding AI Jargon: Speak Like a Pro." If you've ever felt lost in a sea of AI terminology, this section is your life raft. We break down complex terms into snackable, easy-to-digest explanations. By the end of it, you'll be throwing around words like 'neural networks' and 'machine learning' at your next dinner party.

Then, we explore "AI Communities and Resources." Think of it as social networking, but instead of sharing cat videos, you exchange AI insights and breakthroughs. This section is a treasure trove of online forums, courses, and communities where you can mingle with fellow AI aficionados and perhaps find your AI soulmate (in a collaborative project sense).

"Emerging AI Technologies" is where we put on our futuristic goggles and look at what's coming down the tech pipeline. Will we have AI that can taste food? AI that can compose symphonies? Or AI that finally understands why kids don't like broccoli? This section is all about following big things in AI.

In "AI in Open Source: The Power of Collaboration," we celebrate the spirit of sharing and collaboration in the AI world. It's like a potluck dinner, but everyone brings a piece of code instead of a casserole. We delve into how open-source platforms are the playgrounds where today's tech wizards share, collaborate, and create.

"AI Competitions and Challenges" is for those who like a bit of sport with their science. Here, AI is not just a tool; it's a teammate and sometimes an opponent. We look at how AI competitions are not only pushing the boundaries of what's possible but also providing a stage for the brightest minds in AI to showcase their talents.

In "AI Ethics and Governance," we put on our philosopher's hats and ponder the moral maze of AI. This section ensures our AI future is intelligent, wise, and kind. It's like teaching AI how to play chess and the importance of sportsmanship.

"AI and Art and Creativity" is where AI puts on its beret and picks up a paintbrush. We explore how AI is venturing into art and creativity, blurring the lines between human and machine-made art. It's like having a robot Picasso on your computer.

Finally, "The Role of AI in Global Challenges" reminds us that AI isn't just about cool gadgets and intelligent apps. It's a powerful ally in tackling the world's biggest challenges, from climate change to healthcare. This section concerns rolling our digital sleeves and putting AI to work for the greater good.

"AI for the Tech Enthusiast" is a playground for the tech-savvy and the tech-curious alike. The chapter says, "Come for the AI, stay for the amazing possibilities." So, whether you're an AI newbie or a seasoned pro, there's something here to spark your imagination and fuel your passion for AI.

41. **Building Your AI Projects -** It's a fascinating time to be diving into personal AI projects, with resources more accessible than ever before. Open-source platforms like TensorFlow and PyTorch have democratized AI technology, opening a world of possibilities for anyone keen on exploring this field.

These platforms aren't just tools; they're gateways to the vast and dynamic world of AI. With a basic understanding of programming, anyone can start experimenting and building AI models. What makes TensorFlow, PyTorch, and other similar platforms so great are their resources — tutorials that range from beginner to advanced levels and phenomenal community support. Whether it's a question about coding or a request for feedback on a project, the community is there to help. This supportive environment makes it easier for newcomers to navigate the complexities of AI development and gain confidence in their skills.

Personal AI projects can range widely in complexity and application. They are starting with something as simple as a chatbot providing foundational insights into natural language processing. For those who want to dive deeper, tackling more complex applications like image recognition or speech-to-text systems is incredibly rewarding. Not only do these projects enhance technical skills, but they also offer a tangible way to see AI in action.

The key to success in personal AI projects starts with a clear problem statement: what do you want to solve or achieve with your project? Once you have that defined, it's all about experimenting — trying different algorithms, playing with various datasets, and seeing what works and what doesn't. This hands-on experience is invaluable; reading about AI or watching videos is one thing, but applying that knowledge to a practical project brings a different level of understanding.

Engaging in personal AI projects isn't just about building technical skills; it's also about gaining more profound insights on how AI can be applied in real-world scenarios — an opportunity to witness firsthand the potential, the challenges, and the impact of AI technology. And who knows? What starts as a personal project could evolve into something bigger — a startup idea, a research paper, or a unique solution to a pressing problem.

In essence, the world of AI isn't just for experts in tech companies or research labs. Platforms like TensorFlow and PyTorch have become an accessible, exploratory playground for anyone curious and willing to learn. It's a fantastic time to dive into personal AI projects, expand your horizons, and join the exciting AI journey.

42. **Understanding AI Jargon: Speak Like a Pro -** Jargon in AI can be overwhelming. It's like learning a new language. The field contains specialized terms and concepts, like 'neural networks,' 'deep learning,' 'supervised and unsupervised learning,' and 'natural language processing.' These aren't just fancy words; they're the building blocks of AI that anyone interested in the field should learn.

Understanding these terms is crucial it's not just about definitions. It's also about understanding what they mean. For example, when we talk about 'neural networks,' we're talking about systems designed to learn and process information like the human brain does. And then there's 'deep learning.' This subset of machine learning is where these neural networks learn from vast amounts of data. Connecting the dots and understanding how an AI learns and makes decisions is cool.

There are more terms like 'supervised and unsupervised learning,' too. These are different ways of teaching an AI system to do something. In supervised learning, we train it on labeled datasets to make predictions or categorize data. When we use unsupervised learning, it learns from unlabeled data and tries to find patterns and relationships independently.

'Natural language processing' (NLP) is another exciting area. This technology allows machines to understand, interpret, and helpfully respond to human language. The most common examples are chatbots and voice assistants like Siri or Alexa.

The good news is that many online resources are free or low-cost, which can help demystify these terms for beginners. Websites, tutorials, and online classes offer interactive ways for people to learn about AI without prior experience or background knowledge.

And don't forget: every expert was once a beginner, too! So, everyone starts somewhere when learning about AI. There's nothing wrong with not knowing something, so don't let jargon discourage you from exploring AI. With time and effort, things start to make sense. (see Key Terms and Definitions).

43.**AI Communities and Resources -** For anyone entering the world of AI, being part of this community is not just beneficial – it's inspiring and educational.

Platforms like GitHub are goldmines for AI enthusiasts. The amount one can learn by simply exploring all the AI projects and resources that live there is astounding. From beginner-friendly tutorials to advanced applications, these projects give you a practical way to observe AI in action. Additionally, GitHub is a great place to collaborate. Imagine someone halfway across the globe working with you on a project, sharing ideas, and learning from each other. It's a beautiful display of how technology can unite people for a common passion.

Online forums such as Stack Overflow and Reddit's r/Machine Learning are priceless resources. Whether you're stuck on coding, looking for insights on an AI model, or curious about what's currently hot in the field – these platforms provide an endless wealth of information. Community members are typically responsive and knowledgeable, no matter if you're new or experienced.

Attending AI conferences and webinars is another fantastic way to dive headfirst into the field. These events aren't just about listening to experts speak; they're opportunities to engage with content, ask questions, and network with fellow enthusiasts and professionals. They'll also give you a bigger picture of what's happening in AI, such as groundbreaking research and innovative applications.

But being part of the AI community isn't all about learning – it's also about staying motivated and inspired. When starting or hitting some roadblocks in your projects, it's easy to feel overwhelmed. However, when you are part of a community where you can share experiences, successes, and failures– everything becomes more manageable. It reminds you that your journey isn't alone.

The AI community is a dynamic, diverse, and welcoming space full of individuals who share your love for the groundbreaking field. Whether you're chatting online or face to face, the community will accelerate your learning and help you stay connected to AI advancements. It encourages curiosity, fosters collaboration, and celebrates innovation. In other words, it makes diving into AI an exciting and enriching experience.

44. **Emerging AI Technologies -** The rapidly evolving world of AI continues to excite us but also leaves us with numerous ethical dilemmas. Every advancement pushes the boundaries further, leading to new accomplishments we never thought possible.

Take Generative Adversarial Networks (GANs) for example. They've been able to generate highly realistic images and videos. The creations are so lifelike it's hard to believe humans didn't make them. This leap in creativity opens up a whole new plethora of possibilities. We could see new digital art forms or create realistic simulations for training and education. But this exciting technology also has its downsides. You're right about how this opens doors for potential misinformation. Things like media and entertainment could be severely impacted.

Then, we have reinforcement learning, another fascinating area of AI. It's already made headlines with applications like AlphaGo, which mastered complex games only a few years ago. But that was just the beginning. The principles can be applied in several other fields, such as automated trading, where algorithms learn how to make profitable trades independently. Robotics also benefits significantly from this technology because it enables robots to learn and adapt to new tasks through trial and error.

The pace at which AI is evolving means that tech enthusiasts should pay close attention to these emerging technologies. These breakthroughs could quickly revolutionize industries overnight.

Whether it's understanding the latest research, experimenting with new AI tools, or simply staying informed about the latest developments, staying abreast of these changes is critical to grasping the future of technology.

And it doesn't just benefit industry professionals; these advancements will affect us daily. From how we interact with our phones to our approach to solving problems, it has changed drastically since AI started making waves.

This field constantly changes at a blazing speed and holds endless opportunities and challenges. It's not just about witnessing the future unfolding but actively shaping it. The potential to revolutionize various industries and aspects of our daily lives with these emerging AI technologies is immense, and being part of that journey is incredibly exciting.

45. AI in Open Source: The Power of Collaboration - Open source has boosted innovation. It feels like a breath of fresh air in the tech world. It levels the playing field and pushes forward collaboration.

Open-source AI projects bring together minds from all over the world, individuals, and big tech companies working together to improve things. Anybody can help with these projects, whether you're a beginner or an expert; it doesn't matter. The combined effort offers a broader range of perspectives to develop new technologies.

Look at Google's TensorFlow and Meta's PyTorch, for example. They've become iconic tools that are used in AI development worldwide. They owe part of their success to their massive communities of users. In these hubs, developers are busy editing code, fixing bugs, and sharing new ways they have found out of using the software. This environment enriches both programs while providing developers with solid tools and a network that helps them grow.

Another upside is letting people jump into AI development without barriers holding them back. Remember when only those in well-funded labs or big companies could play around with powerful AI tools? These days, they are nearing extinction thanks to open-source platforms. With internet access, anyone can experiment, learn independently, and even help improve these powerhouse tools.

Not only do these platforms breed better technologies, but they also bring together a community that's built off openness, collaboration, and shared progress.

For anyone passionate about AI, engage with open-source projects whenever you can. It isn't just an opportunity to build skills; it allows you to be part of a movement shaping technology's future.

46. **AI Competitions and Challenges** - People find competitions so exciting! They're just as much about education as they are about contests. For instance, competing in a Kaggle challenge is like stepping into an arena where theory meets real-world practice. Here, you can put your skills to work on actual data and complex problems.

Kaggle offers various challenges — from predictive modeling to algorithm development to data analysis — each mimics the problems confronting companies and researchers in everyday work. Whether predicting retail sales or spotting anomalies in medical images, each contest forces you to push the boundaries of what you know and force yourself to apply that knowledge more creatively.

But getting good at AI by tackling competitions isn't just learning how others solve problems. By participating, you also get hands-on experience with many different techniques — trying various things out — and learn how to implement AI models practically. Having a large field of participants makes it easy to get feedback on your approach: By collaborating with others, sharing insights, and seeing new ways to attack the problem from teammates or competitors, you'll expand your horizons faster than if you were working alone.

Excellent performance in Kaggle contests (and other similar ones) can also come with perks beyond prizes. For example, many AI professionals started by doing well in these competitions. Being able to showcase your skill set and quickly build a portfolio around creative applications of complex models is incredibly valuable. It demonstrates that you have the skills required for AI and can think outside standard practices.

And once employers or future collaborators see such achievements on your résumé, they'll already know you're capable of great things in AI.

Competitions aren't products; they're experiences. And when those experiences involve challenges that push what people think is possible with AI, success comes from winning, learning, and networking with others who are just as passionate.

47.AI Ethics and Governance - The role of ethics and governance in AI is a big deal. The ethical implications will become more significant as it becomes more intertwined with our lives.

Ethics is essential because our decisions about our development and deployment today will shape our future. And we don't want to end up in the wrong place, both from a moral and legal standpoint.

The possibilities are endless for AI technologies, which put immense power into shaping our lives via algorithms and decisions made by machines. That's why addressing data privacy, algorithmic bias, and potential misuse is essential.

AI models rely heavily on personal data to function well, if not perfectly. So, finding the equilibrium between using this data without invading people's privacy rights is essential. We must figure out how to protect people while ensuring AI does what it should.

AI systems are only as unbiased as the data they use to learn from. So, when an algorithm makes a decision that reflects prejudices existing in the real world, things can get dangerous quickly. Much is at stake, especially in recruitment, lending, and law enforcement.

Understanding these ethical considerations is vital for anyone involved in AI development. It's not enough to build efficient AI systems — ensuring they're developed responsibly must be on everyone's mind. Guidelines like those set out by the European Union and IEEE provide frameworks that help tech enthusiasts make ethical choices when building or working with AI technologies.

These standards aren't about limiting creativity or innovation but rather about protecting society from the potential negative impacts of AI while still using it for good.

Being familiar with these guidelines ensures that as tech enthusiasts develop or work with AI technologies, they don't only focus on what it can do but also what it should do.

The conversation around AI ethics involves everyone, from developers and companies to regulators, ethicists, and the wider public. It's a dialogue that will only become more important as technology advances to ensure the AI-driven future we're building is safe, fair, and beneficial for everyone.

48. Investing in AI: The Smart Money - If you've both an appreciation for tech and a knack for math, investing in AI technology or startups is a great way to combine the two and make some serious dough. The AI market isn't just growing; it's exploding forward at a considerable rate, brought on by significant investments from venture capitalists and big-name tech companies. This lightning pace of progress and constant development makes it one of the most attractive sectors to be involved in. Startups are popping up daily, offering new takes and applications that are shaking industries from healthcare to retail, and established companies are not far behind them.

At this point, recognizing the potential of AI is easy enough, but getting your hands on any kind of it is much more complicated. Not only do you need a deep understanding of market trends to gauge which tech will pay off in the long run, but understanding the technology itself can also be challenging. It's not all just robots doing work for us, there. There is much more nuance to it.

Understanding what problems new tech can solve and which industries they'll disrupt is critical to making smart money moves here. So, suppose you're serious about joining in on this green gold rush. In that case, you'll have to keep an eye out for new AI technologies whenever they pop up and see where their applications take us — this means following recent developments in research and seeing how these developments can be used in real-world scenarios.

You also need some vision — an ability to know which technologies will become mainstream before they do so you can catch them while they're cheap. And while we're here, why not look at how these advancements might affect society or economies in general?

So, for those of us who know money doesn't grow on trees but instead comes out of ATMs (which are powered by electricity... which is made by humans...), there are loads of opportunities within the world of AI. But it does require a lot of work to get returns on it, especially since we're still figuring out how to use this tech ourselves.

49. **AI in Art and Creativity** - Isn't it fascinating, and a little uncanny, how AI is creeping into the domains of art and creativity? It feels like we're on the cusp of a new era in creative expression, where human and machine-made works are increasingly blurred. Once used strictly for data analysis and problem-solving, AI algorithms now feed images to generate paintings, music notes to make songs, and even text to write stories. It's challenging our idea of what it means to be creative.

Take Google's DeepDream as an example. By tweaking how AI interprets images, DeepDream creates hallucinatory versions that reveal hidden patterns within neural networks. And then there's OpenAI's Jukebox, which generates music in many styles with lyrics to boot. Both projects show us what machines can do and what they can create.

But AI-made art isn't universally accepted. Critics question its authenticity and emotional depth, while supporters consider it a groundbreaking artistic medium. This division makes the intersection of AI and art all the more fascinating because it gets us thinking about creativity itself: What does it mean? Can machines be creative, or are they just extensions of our abilities?

And then there's the question of how artists use AI in their process. Some would say that AI is more like a collaborator than anything else, allowing them to present ideas in new ways and break down creative barriers. Others see it as plain old tools like paintbrushes or instruments, nothing more than aids.

Ultimately, bringing together AI and art isn't just about technology — it's also cultural and philosophical. It has us second-guessing everything we thought we knew about these mediums. But whether you believe that art made by algorithms is accurate artwork or not, you have to admit that this trend is creating so many new paths for creativity that everyone, from artists to musicians, should be excited about exploring further. The space where AI and art overlap is fantastic and filled with possibilities and questions. And being alive to witness it all unfold is a privilege that we shouldn't take for granted.

50. **The Role of AI in Global Challenges -** To solve the world's biggest problems. Artificial Intelligence (AI) can do that, and I don't think people realize that enough. You'd probably think of AI as something like Siri, not a solution to climate change or healthcare issues. However, it's very eye-opening to consider that this technology can be used for more than just searching for dinner recipes. But how?

Well, one example is using data. Climate change is a huge thing that we're all facing, and we need to address it before things get worse. By analyzing data on ocean temperatures, AI models can help us better understand what changes are required to keep our planet intact. It's almost like having your genie that shows you what will happen years from now if we don't act today.

And in healthcare, it has just as big of an impact. The more medical data AI accesses, the easier it is for us to predict diseases and how to treat them. Imagine how many more lives could be saved if AI could detect severe illnesses like cancer or heart disease years before a human doctor could. This would give patients plenty of time to get treatment while they're still healthy – which would significantly increase their odds of survival.

There's so much else that it can do, too, like allocate resources during times of natural disasters or refugee crises so that they reach people who need them most – but at the end of the day, there's one thing that needs to be understood: Although these machines have potential, they're only as good as the humans who use them.

CHAPTER 6
AI FOR THE NON-TECH PROFESSIONAL

In Chapter 6, "AI for the Non-Tech Professional," we take a delightful detour into the world of AI for those who don't speak fluent 'tech-ese.' This chapter is like a friendly translator, turning the complex language of AI into fun, easy-to-understand tidbits. It's perfect for anyone who's ever nodded to a tech conversation while secretly wondering if an algorithm is some exotic dance move.

We start with "AI for Lawyers: Legal Bots," exploring how AI is making its way into courtrooms and legal offices, not as a defendant or lawyer (yet), but as a helpful assistant. Imagine a world where AI helps with legal research but, thankfully, doesn't wear those old-fashioned wigs.

Next, in "AI in Real Estate: Virtual Property Tours," we see how AI is giving real estate a tech makeover. It's like having a super-smart real estate agent who can predict your dream home before you know what you want. Virtual tours and AI-driven market analysis are turning house hunting from a guessing game into a more precise science.

Then, we dive into "AI in Journalism: Automated Reporting." Here, AI takes on the role of a news reporter, minus the fedora and press badge.

We discuss how AI is helping churn out news articles, particularly on topics where speed is critical. It's not quite Lois Lane or Clark Kent, but it's getting there.

"AI for Educators: Personalized Learning" shows how AI is getting a gold star in the classroom. This section is all about AI as a teaching assistant, helping to tailor education to each student's needs. It's like having a tutor who's good at math and doesn't need to sleep or take breaks.

In "AI in Retail: The High-Tech Shop," we explore how shopping has evolved from guessing what customers want to AI-powered personal shopping experiences. It's like having a personal stylist who knows your wardrobe better than you and doesn't judge your fashion choices.

"AI for Artists and Designers: Creative Assistants" delves into the artsy side of AI. AI is the muse that never sleeps here, offering creative suggestions and helping artists and designers push boundaries. It's like collaborating with a robot that's surprisingly good at picking paint colors.

"AI in Sports: Analyzing the Game" takes us into the athletic arena, where AI is the new coach with all the stats. It's crunching numbers, analyzing plays, and maybe one day, it'll even give motivational speeches in the locker room.

"AI for Chefs: Culinary Creations" spices things up by showing how AI enters the kitchen, suggests recipes, and helps chefs create new culinary delights. It's like a sous-chef that knows a million recipes and never accidentally burns the cookies.

"AI in Event Planning: The Perfect Party" reveals how AI is the new party planner on the block, helping organize events with precision and flair. It's like having an excellent personal assistant who organizes parties and doesn't get flustered over last-minute changes.

Lastly, "AI for Farmers: Precision Agriculture" shows how AI is getting its hands dirty in agriculture, helping farmers grow more with less. It's like a high-tech farmer without a straw hat and overalls.

"AI for the Non-Tech Professional" is your go-to guide for understanding how AI changes the game in various non-tech professions. It's like a friendly chat over coffee about how AI is sneaking into all sorts of jobs, making things more accessible, efficient, and futuristic. So, whether you're a lawyer, chef, or anything in between, this chapter has a little AI magic for you – no tech jargon decoder needed!

51. **AI for Lawyers: Legal Bots -** We might be witnessing the digital revolution of a very manual and time-consuming field. And it's not just about streamlining long and tedious processes. AI offers ways to increase accuracy and efficiency, which is invaluable in this sector.

Take legal research, a fundamental part of legal work yet notoriously laborious. But AI tools are changing that; they're transforming law research by sifting through piles of documents, cases, and precedents much faster than any human could hope. It pulled relevant information that would take a person days or weeks in seconds. This doesn't just speed things up but introduces a new level of precision to something once seen as unattainable. Just look at Casetext's CoCounsel; this tool provides lawyers with quick, relevant answers to complex legal questions that can enhance advice and representation quality.

But let's not forget that AI's reach goes beyond research, too. Its use in drafting and reviewing legal documents is vast as well. Contracts, agreements, and similar documents must be accurate and detailed. Something AI can do quite effortlessly to make sure these documents aren't only made efficiently but also without errors. This lightens the load on lawyers so they can focus more on strategic aspects while avoiding expensive mistakes.

Lastly, we have AI's ability to predict case outcomes using previous data. Analyzing how similar cases were settled in the past allows lawyers to understand what will likely happen in their current cases, giving them valuable insights when formulating strategies or advising their clients.

AI isn't just about getting new tech into law firms; it completely changes how work is done, making the process more accessible, efficient, and accurate. It's something that not only benefits lawyers but clients as well. As we continue to improve AI, its role in the field will only become more significant, opening up new and exciting possibilities that will shape the future of legal practice and justice.

52.**AI in Real Estate: Virtual Property Tours** - The real estate industry is changing, and it's all thanks to Artificial Intelligence (AI). The integration of AI has given rise to innovative services — like virtual property tours — completely transforming how we buy, sell, and view properties. And when I say transforming, trust me, I mean it. These AI-driven virtual tours allow potential buyers an incredibly realistic and immersive property experience without being physically there. This is convenient and incredible, especially for situations where physical viewing may be challenging or impossible, like during travel restrictions or for international buyers. Utilizing the force of AI, these virtual tours are more than just simple video walkthroughs; they are interactive, detailed, and can even be customized to the viewer's preferences.

But don't think AI's role in the real estate sector stops at virtual tours. There's so much more this technology can do. Another important factor is its use of automated valuation models (AVMs). These AI algorithms can use extensive market data to analyze various things, such as recent sales, property features, market trends, and more, to estimate a property's value accurately. Ultimately, this benefits buyers and sellers by providing data-driven valuations and precise reports to help them make better decisions when buying or selling properties. It's a massive leap from traditional valuation methods, which can sometimes be time-consuming and subjective.

Companies like Zillow are already off and running by incorporating AI in real estate. They offer tools, including instant home value estimates, which demonstrate the power of efficiency and transparency that comes with AI-assisted valuation processes. This speeds up the process and delivers an impressive level of precision and objectivity that was previously difficult to obtain. As a result, the real estate market is becoming more accessible for everyone because, let's face it… who doesn't want to own property?

53.AI in Journalism: Automated Reporting - AI's impact is palpable. It's altering journalism and the way we tell stories. Seeing a union of human creativity and technology in a newsroom is fascinating. A great example of this is robot journalism or automated journalism, whatever you'd like to call it. As the name implies, it uses AI to automate routine reporting tasks like writing articles about sports results or financial updates.

The speed at which these systems can analyze data and generate coherent fact-based reports is mind-boggling. It isn't just impressive, though — it's incredibly efficient too. Many news organizations have implemented this system to handle mundane reporting tasks rather than using humans. The Associated Press has been at the forefront of automated reports with the help of these AI systems.

The workflow in news organizations is changing due to automation. But AI doesn't just stop there; its role in journalism also extends to investigative purposes. Journalists are now using it to sift through massive amounts of data. These tasks would either take humans ages or be impossible to do effectively.

When used by journalists, AI can quickly sort through vast piles of information and promptly highlight significant bits — something a human could never do without dedicating an absurd amount of time.

But by no means does this mean that humans aren't necessary anymore — they very much are! Freeing human journalists from mundane tasks means they can finally focus on things only they can do, such as investigating pieces, interviews, and creating engaging content.

AI processes data-heavy workloads while humans bring context, understanding, and empathy into their work —the best of both worlds.

Simply put, AI isn't trying to replace journalists with robots that write better articles than us (yet). It's here as an aid – almost like a second pair of eyes used for different purposes.

54. **AI for Educators: Personalized Learning** - AI is transforming how we learn and teach, and it's fantastic to see. These personalized learning experiences that AI enables are revolutionary. Picture a classroom where each student gets an education tailored to them — their learning patterns, strengths, weaknesses, everything. Luckily, AI systems are making this a reality by analyzing how students learn and adapting the educational content accordingly. Because of this approach, students are more engaged in what they're learning and find it more effective when compared to traditional teaching methods that don't account for these steps.

For example, Carnegie Learning is an online platform that uses AI to provide personalized math instruction. The platform adjusts to a student's pace and unique learning style (it's like having a personal tutor). This can make a massive difference in subjects like math or any other issue where students frequently get discouraged.

AI isn't just limited to learning; it also tackles administrative tasks! Grading is a task that can be pretty time-consuming for educators. With the help of AI, this can be done automatically. Hence, teachers have more time to engage with students individually to develop innovative teaching methods or participate in classroom discussions.

But remember that none of this is the peak... we're still on the climb! Efficiency isn't the only thing improving — inclusivity and adaptability, too. You see, new ways of learning will pop up thanks to AI, which will cater to a wide range of learners' abilities and styles, making education accessible for everyone while remaining practical. It's an incredible time in education, and our future is bright with AI leading the way toward genuinely personalized, dynamic learning environments.

55.AI in Retail: The High-Tech Shop - No doubt about it. AI is doing all sorts of crazy things to retail, so it's revolutionary. They are improving the customer experience while making everything run much smoother. The most noticeable thing about AI in retail is how it suggests products to people. These suggestions come from the past purchase history and current browsing of that person. This helps the retailers generate more sales as customers usually get these suggestions and are more likely to buy them. Satisfying both parties here: shoppers find what they need (even if they didn't know they needed it), and retailers get more money.

But aside from that, AI does help in other areas, too! It has a lot on its plate that makes retailing easier for people. One big thing would be inventory management. Figuring out what people want by looking at past data and market trends allows retailers to stock their shelves well enough that there will be neither too much nor too little. This ensures no one gets angry because their favorite snacks are sold out or you don't have any customers come in because your shop is empty.

If you believe only humans can achieve this through observation, think differently. AI employs cameras to track shoppers' interests, yet there are many areas where we still outperform AI, particularly in optimization tasks like marketing. With AI's insights into which store sections draw the most traffic, retailers can strategically place in-demand items in these areas, boosting sales and potentially introducing new products more effectively.

Lastly, you've got Amazon Go Stores, where this whole list comes together into one package. People used to have to stand in line forever to pay for groceries. Now, with AI, customers go around their store picking up food until they have enough and can walk out of the store without waiting in line for anything or anyone.

Seeing what AI has already done for retailing is cool. It's made things much more efficient and personal, benefits both parties, and makes things much more accessible. I'm excited to see what the future holds in this industry as AI continues to grow.

56. AI for Artists and Designers: Creative Assistants - It's like a new dimension where technology meets creativity, and the opportunities seem endless. AI is no longer just here to help with analysis and automation; it's now an essential assistant for artists and designers alike. It is giving us more outlets than ever before.

AI algorithms have been able to generate new design ideas and inspire artistic creations for a while now. This is a game changer since it's like having a partner who never runs out of ideas. Creative professionals can feed concepts into an AI system, and then it'll respond with suggestions that no human would've ever thought of. This can do wonders for creatives! Offering fresh perspectives and new ideas can push work into exciting new directions.

The emergence of AI-generated art is prime proof of this point, too. Platforms like DeepArt are more than just gimmicks; they're powerhouses that offer all sorts of new forms of expression. These platforms use algorithmic magic to make basic images into crazy pieces of art filled with different styles and techniques. This isn't done by copying old art but by making something unique, blurring the line between human and machine creativity.

The design has been hit just as hard as art, too! The process can be super intimidating for designers when choosing color palettes or creating layouts. But thankfully, there's a tool that can help with this, too — AI tools suggest combinations and designs that humans might never think about. It's like having an endless source of inspiration and another set of eyes that see the world differently.

AI in both art and design is truly mind-boggling, though! It's more than just technological advancements; it's pushing creatives and designers to explore unknown territory by blending our intuition with AI power and making mesmerizing pieces, leaving you questioning how they were made and delivering a world of futuristic possibilities. All while showing us that the future can be one where technology and creativity coexist in perfect harmony.

57. **AI in Sports: Analyzing the Game -** AI has revolutionized the sports sector, significantly impacting players, teams, and fans. Its capacity to scrutinize game data for comprehensive insights into player abilities and team tactics is remarkable. It acts like an additional coach, identifying aspects usually unnoticed, aiding teams in making better strategic decisions, and potentially gaining a competitive advantage.

Remarkably, AI's role in injury prevention stands out. Athletes now have AI-enabled wearable devices that track real-time heart rate, oxygen levels, and movements. This wealth of data aids injury prevention by allowing coaches to optimize training and recovery plans.

AI has also transformed the fan experience in sports. Fans now receive customized content based on their preferences, such as highlights of favored players or teams and game predictions that add excitement to viewing. AI-driven platforms offer easy access to detailed information about teams and players, enriching the fans' understanding and enjoyment of the game.

The Wimbledon tournament serves as a prime illustration of AI's effectiveness. There, IBM's Watson provided fans with real-time match insights and in-depth analyses, enhancing their engagement with the game.

AI has significantly influenced the sports industry, from improving performances and preventing injuries to altering how fans engage with their beloved sports. As AI continues to evolve, its role in shaping the future of sports is undeniable, marking an exciting era of innovation and new possibilities in the realm of sports.

58. **AI for Chefs: Culinary Creations -** Isn't what AI can do in the culinary world fascinating? It's like we're living in an age of sci-fi movies. You know, where robots are every day and can serve you a delicious meal at lightning speed.

AI's ability to create new recipes is one of the most exciting features. With the ability to analyze vast amounts of data on flavor profiles and food pairings, AI algorithms can suggest combinations even experienced chefs wouldn't think of. So, you have this innovative culinary mind that keeps giving you new ideas for dishes.

Chef Watson, made by IBM, is a perfect example of this innovation. With only specified ingredients and your preferences, it can generate unique recipes. Chefs use tools like this to experiment with different ingredients and flavors, pushing the boundaries of traditional cooking. But tools like these aren't only suitable for professionals. Imagine being at home and having access to a tool that can suggest recipes based on what you currently have in your kitchen. It's an easy way to get creative in the kitchen without putting much effort into it.

AI also helps restaurant menus by analyzing customer preferences, purchase patterns, and seasonal ingredients. By doing so, restaurants can tailor their menu to their customers' tastes. This improves customer satisfaction and business efficiency since they'll avoid waste if they know certain dishes will be popular.

Predicting food trends is also something AI is great for. AI can identify emerging patterns in consumer preferences and dietary habits through data from various sources. This insight helps restaurants, producers, and grocery stores meet demand more effectively and stay ahead of everyone else.

At its core, AI isn't just technology used for cooking; it's also enhancing creativity, efficiency, and satisfaction. It shows how powerful AI is when you see how it's transforming cooking into exciting ways – even if that means being frustrated over not knowing what recipe you want to cook tonight.

59. AI in Event Planning: The Perfect Party - Indeed, the way AI is changing the game in event planning is genuinely excellent. It's like having an intelligent assistant who makes event logistics simple and adds a personal touch to events, making them more engaging and memorable. Being able to automate everything means that planning an event becomes a lot easier and far less prone to error.

The most exciting part of AI in event planning is how it can personalize experiences for attendees. Imagine walking into an event where everything from the music, lighting, and content is explicitly tailored to your preferences. This level of personalization has become possible thanks to AI tools that analyze attendee data. The goal is always to make each event unique so it resonates with those attending.

Another way event planners can use AI is by predicting when and where an event will do best. Planners can feed historical data and attendee preferences into AI algorithms to predict when and where an event will succeed most. It's insights like this that help maximize attendance and satisfaction.

In marketing, AI has been a massive help for event planners trying to reach their target audience with pinpoint accuracy. Using AI-driven analytics, they've ensured that marketing efforts aren't just broad and practical. Even after an event ends, AI tools can analyze different metrics to measure an event's success. Insights such as these are crucial for improving future events.

Lastly, we have chatbots, which are quickly becoming quite popular in event registration and customer service. They give attendees instant information and assistance, significantly improving their experience throughout the process. When you think about it, it does feel like you're being helped by someone at a desk who's there 24/7.

So when you consider all of these factors — from logistics down to customer service — it's clear how impactful AI has become in events, especially planning. What's even more exciting is thinking about how AI will continue to evolve and transform events in the future.

60. **AI for Farmers: Precision Agriculture** - AI has changed agriculture. It's incredible how this technology has enabled farmers to improve their practices and make agriculture more efficient, sustainable, and productive. One particular groundbreaking concept in farming made possible by AI is precision farming. Powered by AI, it allows for detailed and accurate insights into every aspect of agriculture by analyzing data from various sources such as satellites and drones. This includes optimizing planting schedules, watering regimes, and harvesting times so that every action taken on a farm is as efficient as possible.

The predictability of weather patterns that AI provides is also revolutionary. Farmers can now plan and take measures to prepare for different weather conditions, reducing the risk of crop damage. This was almost unfathomable before sophisticated AI algorithms were developed. Additionally, AI plays an invaluable role in monitoring crop health. By continuously analyzing data on crop conditions, AI can provide early warnings about potential issues like disease or pest infestations so that timely interventions can be made.

AI also offers significant insights into soil management. Knowing the state of soil health is crucial for successful farming because it affects yields significantly. With the help of AI algorithms, soil data can be analyzed to provide recommendations on improving its quality and fertility.

Intelligent farming equipment is one of the most exciting agricultural developments driven by AI. Companies like Blue River Technology are at the forefront of this innovation by using AI to create equipment that can identify and treat weeds precisely — a targeted approach to weed control that significantly reduces herbicide use.

It's easy enough to summarize everything by saying that when it comes down to it, AI in agriculture isn't just about higher yields; it's about radical transformation across the entire industry. From precision farming down to intelligent equipment development — these innovations are what have enabled us to finally see a glimpse at what more efficient, sustainable, and productive agriculture looks like while helping farmers get the most out of their resources, reduce their environmental impact, and meet the growing food demands of the world.

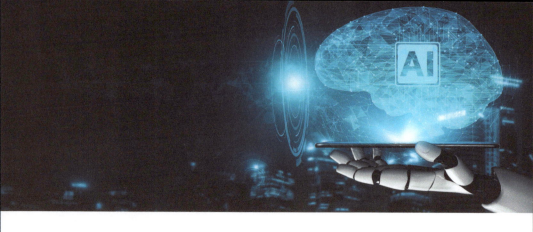

CHAPTER 7
THE DARK SIDE OF AI

Welcome to Chapter 7, "The Dark Side of AI," where we switch on the metaphorical flashlight and explore Artificial Intelligence (AI)'s spookier nooks and crannies. This isn't your typical haunted house tour, but it's got its share of AI skeletons in the closet. Think of it as a friendly warning label on the AI package, saying, "Handle with care, and maybe don't let it babysit your kids just yet."

First, we tackle the tricky topic of AI bias, where sometimes AI prefers certain groups, like a biased judge at a chili cookoff, but with algorithms instead of a spoon. We dive into how these biases can sneak into AI systems and the efforts to teach AI the good manners of fairness and impartiality.

Next, we tiptoe into the realm of privacy concerns, where AI sometimes likes to snoop a little too much. It's like having a nosy neighbor who knows your name, where you live, your favorite pizza toppings, and the last time you binge-watched a TV series. This section discusses the balancing act between leveraging AI for its incredible capabilities and keeping our digital curtains closed.

Then, we discuss job displacement, a scenario where AI might be too good at its job, leading to concerns about unemployment. It's like AI is the overeager intern who accidentally makes the rest of us look a bit unnecessary. We explore the implications of automation and the need for adapting our workforce for the future.

AI in warfare is up next, and it's a bit like opening Pandora's box, but with code and algorithms. The ethical dilemmas of using AI in military applications are discussed, pondering whether handing over life-and-death decisions to machines is wise. Spoiler alert: it isn't straightforward.

Finally, we ponder the AI singularity – the point where AI might outsmart us all. It's like a sci-fi movie plot but with more PhDs and fewer aliens. This section explores the potential future where AI becomes self-aware and hopefully decides to be more like a benevolent ruler than a rogue overlord.

"The Dark Side of AI" of "Bots & Brilliance" is a candid, slightly cheeky look at AI's challenges and ethical considerations. It's a reminder that with great power comes great responsibility (or processing capability). So, buckle up, and let's navigate the darker side of AI, ensuring we use this powerful tool wisely and don't accidentally create a robot uprising.

61. **Bias in AI: Garbage In, Bias Out** - Bias in AI is a huge issue. It's also complex and challenging and speaks to broader societal problems. Since AI systems learn from the data they're given, they tend to mimic any biases lurking in that data. This can lead to severe consequences when these systems are used for facial recognition or credit scoring.

Facial recognition is an obvious case in point: There have been numerous examples of these systems not working as well on people with darker skin or women. That's not just a technical problem — it's a question of fairness and equality. Imagine how things could go wrong if these biases crept into more crucial areas like law enforcement or job recruitment.

Credit scoring algorithms pose a similar problem. Economic biases can muddy the waters, giving inaccurate financial judgments based on information that shouldn't matter. And this has real-world consequences for people, too, potentially making it harder for them to get loans or credit.

This means preventing unfair bias from creeping into AI is crucial! To that end, organizations are working on diversifying training datasets and developing algorithms capable of spotting and fixing biases. Diversifying the training data will help us build AI that inclusively represents the natural world and its populations. As for detecting and minimizing biases, those algorithms are critical to ensuring the technology operates fairly and ethically.

This stuff isn't easy! Biases can be problematic to find in data because they're so deeply ingrained — sometimes, they're just reflections of long-standing societal biases nobody ever noticed! That's why everyone involved will need continuous effort to sort and fix these biases.

Combating AI bias isn't just a matter of tech know-how; it's also about society itself. It needs multiple fields of study and a collective commitment to fairness and equality. AI will continue to become more important in our lives in the future, so we can't afford just to let these biases slide. It's about using our intelligence to create intelligent systems that are also fair and just.

62. **Privacy Concerns: Big Brother AI -** The privacy implications of AI integration into our daily lives can be concerning. It's an issue that's becoming increasingly urgent as these systems become more advanced and widespread, and it's at the core of what makes them so powerful: data. AI systems often collect and process enormous amounts of information, including sensitive Personally Identifiable Information (PII), prompting fears over surveillance and potential misuse.

The Cambridge Analytica scandal made this painfully clear. It showed how personal data can be abused — in this case, for political advertising purposes — with information harvested from platforms like Facebook, which many people use daily without realizing its actual threats. In an era where personal data can be used to influence and deceive, it pays to be worried.

We've already seen steps towards addressing this concern by introducing regulations like Europe's General Data Protection Regulation (GDPR). GDPR gives individuals more control over their data and imposes strict rules on those who collect and process it, effectively laying the groundwork for similar initiatives in other regions.

However, leveraging AI for all its benefits while keeping personal privacy intact is also complicated. On the one hand, we have the power to make significant advancements in healthcare, education, transportation, and much more through AI. On the other hand, lies a critical concern: ensuring these advancements don't infringe on personal rights.

Finding that balance will require continued effort from policymakers, tech companies, AI developers, and the public. They'll need to collaborate on developing secure systems that respect user privacy while remaining transparent about how they use data — not to mention regularly updating regulations as technology progresses.

The end goal is simple. We should strive to create AI that helps society flourish without putting individual rights at risk. Easier said than done? Of course! But essential work must be done if we want to see responsible advancements in technology as we advance.

63. **Job Displacement: The Robot Took My Job! -** Touching on the point of modern society. The automation that AI and robotics bring is indeed a double-edged sword. On the one hand, these technologies are making giant leaps in efficiency and productivity. It transformed industries in ways we couldn't fathom two decades ago and raised huge concerns about job displacement. You will likely see the most traditional reliance on human labor in manufacturing, customer service, and transportation.

Take a look at manufacturing, for example. Robots and AI systems can perform tasks more quickly and accurately than human workers. This raises productivity but also raises concerns about the potential reduction in the number of jobs available.

Next up is customer service; with the help of chatbots and virtual assistants powered by AI, they can handle a wide range of customer queries, reducing the need for human customer service reps.

Finally, we have transportation where self-driving vehicles change the drivers' landscape entirely.

Preparing the workforce for this shift will be challenging. But it's not impossible. Reskilling and education will be crucial for getting everyone ready for this new world where AI runs rampant. And we're not just talking about technical skills; adapting your thinking and solving problems will also be critical abilities that you should hone.

But there's also good news! The rise of AI provides new job opportunities as well! Fields like AI development, data analysis, and machine learning offer exciting careers that proliferate.

The transition for those displaced from traditional roles is tricky, though. Acquiring new skills isn't enough to ensure success in this new era. You'll need to adapt entirely to an environment much different than you were used to before.

Governments will have their work cut out for them when developing programs, but it won't be impossible. Lifelong learning policies, retraining programs, Career counseling,

These can help bridge the gap separating the old and new job markets.

We should also work to foster a culture of continuous learning and adaptability. Getting people ready for a future where change is all that matters.

It all boils down to this. Although AI and robotics make things more complicated regarding job displacement, they still offer opportunities to grow and innovate. Keeping these two aspects balanced is critical to ensuring that we reap the benefits of AI and robotics while supporting those impacted by its changes. It's a complex issue but one that we have to address head-on.

64. **AI and Warfare: Ethical Dilemmas** - The use of AI in warfare raises profound questions about how we fight and the role of technology in life-and-death situations. Autonomous weapons systems that can operate without human intervention could dramatically change how warfare has been conducted for centuries, and it's right to ask hard questions about it.

The primary worry with these systems is that they will make decisions — like who to kill — without human oversight. It's an understandably unnerving prospect, the possibility of ceding power over life and death to machines. Using AI weapons risks new forms of military escalation and civilian harm if misused. Modern battlefields are chaotic places, and war is by nature unpredictable, so it would be challenging to ensure that these systems could tell the difference between things they should shoot — like bombs or guns — and things they shouldn't, like civilians or other innocents.

Of course, all these issues are well understood by governments worldwide. The United Nations Conventions on Certain Conventional Weapons (CCW) have been crucial for discussing lethal autonomous weapons systems. These meetings have brought together states and non-governmental organizations with a range of perspectives to work through the complex implications of this technology.

There is growing support among nations (and within some militaries) for pre-emptive bans on fully autonomous weapons systems. Many believe that the risks are too significant and that ethical decision-making in warfare requires humans in the loop.

Others counterargue that AI could make warfare more precise and less destructive. Properly regulated development could lead to more targeted engagements with fewer unintended consequences.

These disagreements reflect how quickly our world changes due to emerging technologies such as AI. And since change happens at an increasingly rapid pace, there's no time like today to try and draw lines around what we're willing to do now and what we're not.

65. The AI Singularity: Sci-Fi or Future Reality? - The idea of the

AI singularity is captivating. It's one of those things you can't help but think about, and it's a topic that has sparked endless debates about the future of technology and humanity. When you think about it, it sounds like something straight out of a sci-fi movie. But the thing is, some of our most brilliant minds are taking this theory very seriously.

When we talk about singularity, we mean when a machine surpasses human intelligence and becomes capable of self-improvement; this concept alone is enough to simultaneously get people excited yet terrified.

On one hand, some people see the singularity as a game-changer for technology. If AI gets to the point where it can improve itself without any help from humans, then all bets are off on what we could accomplish as a species. Problems like climate change or curing diseases would no longer be considered "problems" because super-intelligent AI could fix them instantly. The potential benefits that come with reaching this level of AI are unimaginable.

However, on the other hand, valid concerns have been raised about what could happen if we got to this point in AI development. For starters, losing control over these super-intelligent systems sounds pretty scary if you ask me. Predicting or controlling their actions would be impossible if machines surpass human intellect. Elon Musk and Stephen Hawking have both voiced their concerns over the advancement of AI, and they fear that if proper regulation isn't put in place, superintelligent AI could lead us down a path of destruction.

The argument for and against singularity continues today, and what's clear is that it doesn't seem like anyone will be changing their stance anytime soon. But I think that despite what side you stand on, there needs to be more serious conversations on how exactly we plan to develop AI that works in our favor. As technology evolves, these discussions will become increasingly necessary and help us build a path forward for AI that brings out the best in humanity while minimizing risks.

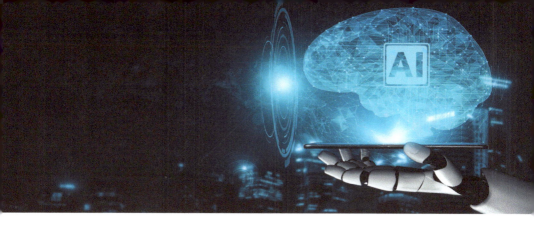

CHAPTER 8
THE FUTURE OF AI

In Chapter 8, "The Future of AI," we strap on our virtual reality goggles and take a whimsical yet insightful ride into the not-so-distant future of Artificial Intelligence (AI). This chapter is akin to a time machine, offering a peek into a world where AI is not just a buzzword but a buddy in our daily adventures. It's a blend of educated guesses, hopeful aspirations, and a dash of sci-fi flavor, making it a delightful read for anyone curious about what tomorrow might hold for AI – and whether or not robots will finally make our coffee just as we like it.

We start by launching into the cosmos with AI as our co-pilot, exploring how it might transform space exploration. Imagine AI systems navigating us to Mars or helping us chat with extraterrestrial beings (hopefully, they're friendly and as curious about us as we are about them). This section looks at the current role of AI in space technology and extends its trajectory to more star-studded parts in the future.

Then, we take a quantum leap into AI and quantum computing. Here, we ponder over AI systems so robust that they make our current smartphones resemble ancient abacuses. This chapter discusses how the fusion of AI with quantum computing could lead to solutions for problems that today's computers might take centuries to solve – like how to fold a fitted sheet perfectly.

Next, we navigate the green pastures of sustainability, where AI is the new superhero in the fight against climate change. From optimizing energy use to helping us grow veggies in our backyard, AI could be our key ally in keeping the planet green and our skies blue. This section is a hopeful look at how AI might help us clean up our act for a greener Earth.

Ethical AI takes center stage as we contemplate a future where AI might have to decide between right and wrong. This part is a bit like teaching a robot not to eat the last cookie – it's about instilling values and ensuring AI plays friendly and fair in a human-centric world.

Finally, we zoom out to a global view of the AI race, where countries are sprinting (or maybe hoverboarding) toward AI supremacy. This section explores the geopolitical tango over AI, pondering whether it will be a cooperative dance or a bit of a toe-stepping boogie.

"The Future of AI" is not just a chapter; it's a playful yet profound journey into AI's possibilities. It's for anyone who's ever wondered whether AI will someday make their bed or if it'll remind them to call their mom. So, buckle up and enjoy the ride into the future – where AI is not just a tool but a character in the story of our lives.

66. **AI and Space Exploration: The Final Frontier -** We're at the dawn of a new era of understanding and exploring the universe. The ability of AI to analyze all that information changes the game; in fact, it could be outright called a revolution. The amount of data collected during space exploration is so significant that it's easy for any human to get overwhelmed. So, processing and making sense of this information is critical when learning new things.

Take NASA's rovers on Mars, for example. AI has allowed these rovers to analyze data, rocks, and soil and decide where to go. This level of independence was something no one thought would be possible a few decades ago. But look at us now! We're learning more about Mars every day.

The beauty of AI is that it can also be used in other types of space missions. For instance, processing and interpreting data from telescopes and satellites helps identify bodies in space, understand cosmic occurrences, and even search for signs of life outside our planet.

As we move into the future of better technology, you can bet that AI will play a big part in managing life on other planets, helping build space stations, and even finding life beyond Earth itself.

For instance, during missions designed to find extraterrestrial life - AI could very well notice if a particular planet or moon has what it takes to house a living thing. In habitats outside our world, however - These systems could monitor resources, manage emergencies, and keep an eye on support systems.

AI isn't just a tool here; It's doing its fair share of daily pushing us past our boundaries. With eyes on far-out-reaching planets and telescopes that never stop looking - We understand more than ever, which is exciting.

67. **Quantum Computing and AI: Supercharged Brains -** Quantum computing combined with AI is fascinating, and the potential behind it is enormous. What we're witnessing now is the beginning of a revolution, which can only be likened to opening the door to a realm of possibilities once seen only in science fiction movies. With quantum computing's incredible ability to perform complex calculations faster than classical computers ever could, we're at the tip of an iceberg when it comes to understanding how it can supercharge our AI algorithms.

When you start combining these two powerhouses, imagine what you can do. Take drug discovery, for example. Scientists would kill (not actually), but they'd do whatever they could for access to this kind of technology. Through simulation and analysis of molecular structures, researchers can find new drugs much faster than ever before. This speed could save millions of lives by getting critical medications into the market that are more accessible than current methods allow.

Implications are just as significant in materials science, too. Atomic-level modeling through quantum computing could lead to the creation of new materials with unique properties. Material like this could change everything from renewable energy to car fuel efficiency.

Large-scale financial systems and climate modeling are another area where quantum AI will shine brightest. We can't see far enough ahead into the future for accurate predictions. But with quantum computing, things can change, giving us once-impossible insights.

The research needed to make this happen isn't easy, though; companies like Google or IBM work tirelessly on projects like this daily to unlock humanity's next step forward. The amount of ways quantum AI could be used is endless.

No matter the application, though, it's clear that the future will be paved with more advanced technologies than ever before. As time passes, there's no doubt that some wild breakthroughs beyond what we could imagine will come out of this field.

68. **AI and Sustainability: Saving the Planet -** AI's role in fighting climate change to live sustainably is both important and impressive. It's like we've given ourselves a superpower that allows us to tackle some of the biggest challenges we've ever faced. You can think of AI as a tool that helps scientists and researchers understand the effects of certain things on our climate. And by understanding the impact, we can put measures in place to prevent or fix them. These models are essential in guiding policy decisions and climate action plans at both local and global levels.

Another thing that makes AI great is how much it's helping us optimize energy usage with little effort. AI-driven systems can manage industry operations to increase efficiency while reducing waste and carbon footprints. This saves money for businesses and is environmentally friendly. Intelligent AI systems control lighting, heating, and cooling in homes, ensuring energy is used efficiently while reducing consumption and lowering utility bills.

You'd be shocked at how much AI has changed agriculture. Sustainable farming practices are a significant factor involved in managing climate change, as well as any other problem tied to it. From using algorithms that help improve crop yields and reduce the need for harmful chemicals to precision farming techniques — which minimize waste and optimize resource use by cutting back on fertilizer —you'll find plenty of ways AI is helping make farming more sustainable.

One of the more exciting areas where AI shines brightly is its ability to monitor wildlife populations. People are using this technology now to track illegal logging or poaching activities, while others use it to predict environmental disasters so they can prevent them altogether. All of this monitoring helps protect ecosystems, which preserves the diversity of life on our planet.

AI isn't just a fantastic new futuristic tool — it's beneficial in preserving Earth's beauty with less work needed from us. The potential for what this system can do is still growing every day, but what we're seeing now is impressive and by no means the end.

69. **Ethical AI: Teaching Right from Wrong -** Our reliance on AI is growing exponentially, so we must ensure that these systems are developed and used ethically. Ethical AI creates designs that quickly make correct decisions and do so somewhat transparently and accountable. We need to be able to strike this balance if we want these technologies to work.

Tackling bias is a massive part of making sure AI stays ethical. Because we've seen that it can unknowingly amplify preexistent societal biases when they aren't adequately designed or monitored. Constantly evaluating and refining the algorithms is critical in avoiding discriminatory outcomes. And it's crucial if we want the public's trust and the benefits of AI for everybody.

We also have privacy concerns with AI processing vast amounts of personal data. There's a chance for individual privacy intrusion, so companies must implement strong measures to protect personal information at all costs.

As powerful as these AI systems become, their potential misuse grows, too. This could include autonomous weapons, deepfakes, or even manipulating financial markets. Developing robust legal frameworks and international agreements is mandatory to prevent harmful uses like those above.

The guidelines provided by the European Union are crucial steps towards establishing frameworks for responsible development and deployment of AI technologies. They serve as a framework for developers and policymakers to create beneficial and safe technologies.

AI has been integrated into nearly every sector already, so while being late, it's better late than never when addressing ethics around them now rather than later on when it's already deeply rooted in our lives.

70. **The Global AI Race: Nations in Competition** - AI is becoming a critical competition domain between nations. It's fascinating and sometimes disconcerting how AI is not just a technological race but also an element of economic and geopolitical power struggles. This competition for AI dominance involves technological advancement, securing economic advantages, and asserting geopolitical influence.

The United States, China, and European Union member states are at the forefront of this race. Each bloc has its approach to AI development and regulation. The U.S., for instance, has a strong culture of innovation driven by its tech giants and research institutions. China has made AI a national priority with significant government support and ambitious plans to be a world leader in AI by 2030. The European Union focuses on driving technological advancements and ethical aspects to create responsible and human-centric AI to be an AI leader.

While this global race undeniably drives fast advancements in AI technology, it raises several essential concerns. One of the most pressing issues is its possible militarization. As nations compete for AI supremacy, there's a possibility that these technologies will be utilized and developed for military purposes, which raises important ethical and security questions. The prospect of autonomous weapons and AI-driven surveillance systems emphasizes the need for international norms and regulations regarding using AI in military/security contexts.

This competition also highlights the importance of international cooperation and law. Since AI technologies are progressively becoming more powerful & pervasive, nations need to work together to form guidelines/agreements that guarantee responsible development/use of AI. Privacy issues arise as these technologies gain potency; addressing problems such as bias & digital division ensures equitable sharing of benefits worldwide.

This competition is complex on various levels. It pushes technology breakthroughs & economic growth while simultaneously forcing us to address challenges through cooperation/international dialogue - like balancing innovation with ethical considerations/security concerns to guarantee humanity benefits from the race. It's an exciting yet complex time in AI but also holds great potential for broad advancements and even greater responsibilities.

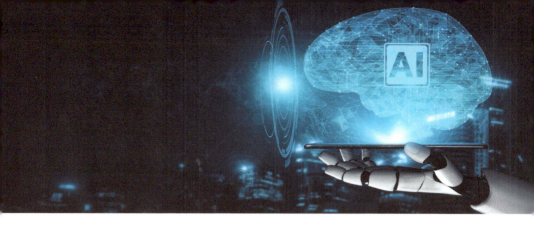

CHAPTER 9
AI AND MANAGEMENT

Welcome to Chapter 9, "AI and Management," where we swap out our tech hats for managerial caps (which, admittedly, are less geeky but just as stylish). This chapter is like a survival guide for managers navigating the wilds of the AI jungle. It's for those who think, "So, I have this team, and now there's AI. What next?"

We start with "AI for Managers: Decision Support Systems," exploring how AI can be the Robin to your managerial Batman. It's all about AI helping you make decisions that are not just good but 'AI-just-read-a-million-data-points' good. Imagine having a sidekick that can crunch numbers without breaking a sweat (or needing coffee breaks).

Next, in "AI and Employee Training: Customized Learning Paths," we dive into how AI revolutionizes employee training. It's like having a personal trainer for each employee, but one more focused on upskilling than burpees. This section shows how AI can tailor training programs to individual needs, making 'one-size-fits-all' a thing of the past.

"AI in Team Collaboration: Smarter Workflows" discusses how AI can be the ultimate team player, streamlining communication and automating the mundane. It's like having an ultra-efficient colleague who never forgets a deadline and doesn't engage in office gossip.

Then, we tackle "AI and Business Strategy: Predictive Analytics." Here, AI steps into the boardroom, helping to shape business strategies with its predictive prowess. It's like a crystal ball but less mystical and more data-driven.

In "AI in Supply Chain Management: The Efficient Chain," we see how AI is like the orchestra conductor for the supply chain, ensuring everything runs harmoniously. This section explores how AI can predict supply chain disruptions before they throw a wrench in the works.

"AI and Corporate Governance: Risk Management" shows how AI can be the lookout on your corporate ship, scanning the horizon for risks and icebergs (or market shifts and compliance issues, which are slightly less dramatic but equally important).

"AI in Sales: The Ultimate Salesperson" reveals how AI can help close deals by analyzing customer data and providing insights that would make even the most seasoned salesperson raise an eyebrow.

In "AI and Corporate Social Responsibility," we discuss how AI can help companies be profitable but also ethical and responsible. It's like having a conscience, but one that analyzes data and trends.

"AI in Talent Acquisition: The Smart Hire" looks at how AI transforms recruitment, making it less about gut feelings and more about insights and analytics. It's like a matchmaker but for job roles and candidates.

Finally, "AI and Workplace Automation: The Good, the Bad, and the Ugly" delves into the complexities of automation. It's about balancing efficiency with empathy, ensuring that while machines take on more tasks, the human spirit in the workplace isn't lost.

"AI and Management" is for the managers who find themselves at the intersection of people and technology, offering insights, laughs, and wisdom on leading teams in the age of AI. It's about embracing the future without losing the human touch. So, grab your managerial toolkit (and maybe a cup of AI-brewed coffee), and let's dive into the art of managing in AI.

71. **AI for Managers: Decision Support Systems** - AI is changing how management works. It's revolutionary; the systems can make decisions like humans but way faster. AI-driven decision support systems are vital to keeping up in fast-moving environments like business. AI can look through and go over massive amounts of data, which a human would take forever to find little tidbits that we would've never found. These systems use advanced predictive abilities that allow them to predict what might happen in the future with a high degree of accuracy. This will enable them to think ahead and make strategies ahead of time.

Now let's get into some examples because I know you got bored there for a second. IBM's WatsonX Analytics is a fantastic example; even if you don't know, this stands out among other AI-driven management solutions. Using it, managers can dig as deep into their business data as they want, like those who dig straight down in Minecraft until they hit lava-ish (we all do it). They also have these advanced predictive models that help managers see into the future and plan for what might happen next.

Using AI to manage things is a big deal. That's not just my opinion either; it's a fact. Decisions used to be made based on nothing but human intuition and limited data analysis. No one says those things aren't good or helpful, but the problem is when you don't have enough information, you tend to make mistakes. That's where AI comes into play: making better decisions with mounds of accurate data. Letting businesses know their options and how each will turn out is everything you could ask for from an assistant.

The results from this technology are huge and worth every penny spent on them, too! You're no longer stuck using your gut feelings (even though some people swear by them) or using old data that doesn't help anymore. With AI, businesses can make intelligent choices that align with their goals and the market. Because of this, outcomes will go through the roof! You'll see efficiency, customer happiness, and a massive boost in profit. So, as I said before, AI isn't just some tool to throw in your back pocket for safekeeping; it's becoming the whole strategy, basically, everything you could ask for in a management system.

72. **AI and Employee Training: Customized Learning Paths -** How AI shapes employee training is mind-blowing. The old one-size-fits-all method companies used is becoming a thing of the past. People can now create their own personalized learning experience thanks to AI systems. Some may be skeptical and wonder how that's possible. Well, all you've got to do is have these systems assess each individual's skill level and learning style. By doing this, programs can accurately tailor the training for each person's needs. That way, they'll be engaged and find the content valuable as it's meant for them specifically.

Companies like Coursera and Udacity are already leading this revolution by using AI in their platforms. They give users a unique path to follow rather than just a generic course everyone takes together. This customization makes learning efficient and impactful for employees. They can develop skills that contribute directly to their role in the company or future career ambitions.

This new method of training doesn't just benefit workers; it also helps organizations tremendously. Businesses can expect a more skilled workforce when investing in these AI-driven platforms. A team constantly improving their skills makes them adaptable, innovative, and better at overcoming modern business challenges. Another perk is boosting employee satisfaction by showing commitment to their growth through personal training opportunities. Showing loyalty has proven time and time again to lead to higher engagement from employees, which shows in productivity levels.

AI in training isn't just another tech slot used by human resources teams everywhere; it's an investment into what matters - people.

73. AI in Team Collaboration: Smarter Workflows - It's incredible how team collaboration tools streamline communication and ensure things are faster and more efficient. When you think about the typical workflow in almost every single team, it involves coordination, communication, and task management. This is where AI steps in to make a significant difference.

AI-driven project management tools, for example, are not just digital to-do lists. They're intelligent systems capable of assigning tasks, setting realistic deadlines, and predicting potential project bottlenecks. So, what does this mean? Teams can address any possible problems before they turn into actual issues that prevent them from progressing with their work. This alone makes the tools valuable. And wait till I tell you what else they once ongoing projects can start feeding the system's data that help them learn even more.

Slack and Microsoft Teams, on the other hand, have become so much more than just places for teams to communicate and work together. With the integration of AI, their utility has skyrocketed. Automated meeting scheduling is an absolute godsend because finding times that work for everyone can be tricky. I'm sure you've been through this before. Additionally, intelligent search within conversations is pretty game-changing, too, since it allows team members to find important information from past discussions rather quickly — something that helps save some valuable time.

By taking care of all these mundane tasks and administrative aspects of work, AI allows team members to spend more time doing core tasks that require attention to detail, creativity, and strategic thinking, which boosts productivity a lot — not to mention job satisfaction as well.

The integration of AI into team collaboration tools isn't just about making things easier either; it's about wholly transforming how teams operate on a day-to-day basis — how they communicate with one another, manage tasks, and solve problems together... all while trying to keep things fun for everyone at the same time because no one wants a dull work environment.

74.AI and Business Strategy: Predictive Analytics - The impact of AI on business strategies, especially with predictive analytics. This technology is no longer an add-on to existing tools but changes how businesses think and operate. Thanks to its algorithms, AI can analyze and make sense of massive amounts of data like historical information, current market trends, and consumer behavior patterns. As a result, it can predict future market conditions with a precision that used to be unimaginable.

Just think about the power of being able to see into the future. Companies can use that gift to make way more strategic moves and not just reactive ones. It's like seeing what will happen in six months while your competitors are still lost in the present. This kind of foresight means businesses can adapt their strategies in advance and often stay ahead in their markets compared to others that might be slower or more focused on reacting after something has changed. In today's fast-paced business world, this is a huge advantage.

Netflix is an excellent example of how this works. The company doesn't use AI only to recommend movies; it uses AI to shape its entire content strategy. By analyzing viewer preferences and other market trends, Netflix makes intelligent choices about what content they should produce or buy from different creators. They don't just throw darts at stuff; they take significant calculated risks with actual underlying data, which has helped them stay strong in the competitive streaming space.

And that's another thing about AI: it works for almost anything you can think of. Retail, finance, healthcare, entertainment...you name it — there are always relevant insights from predictive analytics that businesses can benefit from today and later when new market demands arise.

Artificial Intelligence (AI) is not just about taking over jobs; it fundamentally changes how we do business. Whether it's understanding complex customer behaviors or making strategic decisions based on rock-solid predictions, the role of AI in shaping business strategies is not just important; it's essential. In a world where everything constantly changes, businesses that want to survive can't afford to ignore this tool.

75. **AI in Supply Chain Management: The Efficient Chain –** AI has a transformative effect on supply chain management. It is incredible to see how it optimizes logistics, inventory management, and demand forecasting. Its use in supply chains isn't just a trend; it's necessary for businesses that want to stay competitive.

As I said earlier, logistics is where we see AI shine. The algorithm can accurately predict disruptions and suggest solutions when analyzing all the data. That kind of foresight can save companies from headaches and delayed operations.

Inventory management is the same way. The system will know exactly what needs to be stocked and when without wasting money or space. This is vital; overstocking ties up capital, while understocking can lead to lost sales.

Companies like UPS and FedEx have been using AI in logistics for years. They mainly optimize delivery routes by considering traffic patterns, weather conditions, vehicle capacity, and delivery times. With AI, they can reduce operational costs and make faster deliveries for better customer satisfaction.

If you think that's exciting, look at how AI improves efficiency overall in supply chain management. By improving efficiency, we also make the entire process more resilient in every region.

But ultimately, AI does one thing: it helps companies navigate the complexities in our global economy. It'll make operations more efficient, making it easier to adapt as needed and focus on customers — this will help us build more innovative supply chains for the future instead of just trying to keep up with trends.

76. **AI and Corporate Governance: Risk Management -** AI can be used in corporate governance, especially regarding risk management. It's incredible how AI systems have made themselves so valuable in this area. With all the risks businesses face today, monitoring, analyzing, and dealing with them efficiently is necessary for survival and overall success.

AI systems are perfect for this role since they can process and analyze massive amounts of data quickly and accurately compared to humans. This ability is crucial when dealing with dynamic risks like market volatility, regulatory changes, and cybersecurity threats that fluctuate and often catch us off guard. For example, market volatility looks at investment decisions and financial planning, while regulatory changes might affect compliance and operational processes. Cybersecurity threats, which are growing more complex by the day, pose an immense danger not just to a company's data but also to its reputation and customer trust.

As it stands now, AI can provide continuous monitoring and real-time analysis. It can ransack news feeds, financial reports, regulatory updates, plus online data for potential risks that may not seem threatening at first glance. This new approach to risk management is a game changer. It helps companies identify problems before they become problematic, giving them time to apply necessary countermeasures that could save them from significant losses or damages in the future.

Given these advantages, AI-driven risk management tools are becoming less of a luxury and more of a necessity, considering how confusing today's business environment has become. With the global economy being interconnected, among many other things, we now face risks of greater magnitude than ever before in history. Although it does help corporations deal with these risks as they arise, AI also helps anticipate them and put countermeasures in place beforehand, which is crucial for long-term stability.

In short, AI changes risk management from reactive to more proactive. The goal isn't just trying our best to deal with problems as they come but also predicting and preparing for them. In a world where change is our only constant, AI undoubtedly plays a role in corporate governance and risk management. It gives corporations an edge that helps them stay strong and grow no matter what hurdles they face while being on their feet in the ever-changing business landscape.

77. **AI in Sales: The Ultimate Salesperson -** AI is the transformation of the sales industry. It is a game changer. How it looks into customer behavior and preferences to give valuable insights revolutionizes how we've made sales traditionally. It's like having a crystal ball into what customers want and need.

Take AI-powered sales tools, for example. You can spot potential leads by analyzing customer data and suggesting custom sales strategies to them. This trumps the one-size-fits-all tactic we've all known in the past. A more personalized approach helps customers feel more understood and valued, which is crucial in today's market, where they expect businesses to understand their needs.

Then chatbots and virtual assistants have become so handy in dealing with first-time customer inquiries. They filter and qualify leads before handing them down to human sales reps. That automation simplifies the process, making it quicker and more effective. It also lets teams focus on high-quality leads rather than wasting time on those going nowhere.

Customer experience also gets a big boost from this technology. Just think about being greeted by a chatbot with quick responses while understanding your needs and taking you through a personalized buying journey. That kind of service can significantly improve satisfaction and loyalty.

Salesforce's Einstein AI is an excellent example of this transformation. Using data-driven insights, its tool equips teams to make smarter choices when building customer relationships. Using AI, Salesforce offers a better understanding of customer needs and future trend predictions to craft strategies that work with their target audience.

AI doesn't just help us sell; it helps us understand better, too. Assisting customers in connecting by providing solutions aligned with their needs sets modern from traditional sales strategies apart. In a world where personalization is king, AI isn't just helpful — it's a must-have component as we evolve our tactics in selling things.

78. **AI and Corporate Social Responsibility -** The role of AI in achieving CSR goals is extraordinary. It's interesting to see how technology is helping businesses become more ethically responsible. In a time when our environmental concerns are at an all-time high, it's good to know we have a tool like AI on our side.

It can do things that would take people immense time and energy to achieve. When you hand it Environmental, Social and Governance (ESG) data, it swirls the information around in its head until it has a grip on your ethical and environmental impact. This wasn't easy to calculate, but today, it's easier than ever.

Take carbon footprints, for example; with AI, you'll get real-time insights into the environmental impact you've made so far. This is great because if companies want to start contributing positively towards climate change, they'll have a much better understanding of how much they need to reduce their carbon emissions.

AI helps achieve social impact as well. It can look at employment practices and community engagement activities, giving companies a clear view of their social responsibility.

When talking about governance, AI makes sure companies are staying within regulations. It does this by monitoring internal processes and ensuring nothing shady is happening behind closed doors. In today's world, where every little thing goes viral in seconds, this aspect of AI should not be taken lightly.

This new way of tackling CSR will do one major thing: ensure that brands close the gap between profit and purpose. If done right, Companies will realize they can be successful without damaging society or the environment.

AI is changing the game for how companies approach CSR. It's not just about meeting requirements anymore; this plays a part, but with that kind of power, you can't just stop there... It would be best to keep going until you've made your brand as ethical as possible.

79. **AI in Talent Acquisition: The Smart Hire** – AI significantly impacts talent acquisition. The truth is, it's a game changer. It's giving the hiring process a facelift and making it more efficient and effective. Traditional hiring methods are getting the boot because of their ineffectiveness.

Sifting through resumes and conducting interviews to find potential candidates has become ancient with the rise of AI technology. Nowadays, algorithms can scan resumes quickly and efficiently, and not only that, but they can also understand what sets someone apart. With the context and nuances of someone's experience and skills, these algorithms can sort out people who may be better suited for other roles or even those who might have the potential to do well in their current positions. Once upon a time, this level of analysis was too time-consuming, but now, thanks to AI, we can do it in no time.

As I just mentioned, AI algorithms work quickly; speed is the name of the game here. Not only does it work at a fast pace, but its accuracy is uncanny as well. And these assessment tools evaluate every aspect there is to assess a candidate. Skills? Yes. Personality traits? Also, yes! By doing so, companies can see if someone fits their company culture rather than just looking good on paper. In today's industry, everyone on your team must share values and an ethos; they must resonate with each other.

LinkedIn uses AI technology in its recruitment process, too! Their system doesn't just recommend jobs to candidates based on their profiles; it suggests potential candidates to recruiters based on job requirements! This two-way matching system changed everything for LinkedIn when it came out. Rather than finding opportunities solely for job seekers, their recruiters were able to find talent that would have otherwise been overlooked or lost in a sea of resumes.

The most exciting thing about AI tech in this space, however, is that it can reduce biases that come with hiring. AI algorithms can be built to focus on skills and qualifications without being influenced by racist, sexist, or ageist factors. Focusing solely on what matters in a potential candidate allows for a more diverse workforce, ultimately leading to a more inclusive work environment.

Simply put, the way we hire has changed forever. Gone are the days of manual labor when it comes to recruitment. A data-driven, efficient, and unbiased process is now what employers use when looking for candidates. And as the job market continues to evolve, AI will always be there to connect talent with opportunities.

80. AI and Workplace Automation: The Good, the Bad, and the Ugly

- Although AI-driven automation leads to high efficiency and cost savings, it raises concerns about job displacement and employee morale—the classic double-edged sword of technological advancement.

Automation can make specific roles obsolete, especially those involving repetitive or simple tasks. This can be quite unsettling for the workforce because it's not just the loss of jobs they're scared of. The fear of being replaced by an algorithm or robot renders their skills useless. With this shift comes a new demand for retraining and learning new skills. Companies must invest in learning so that employees can adapt to the ever-changing job landscape. This will help keep them valuable in the company's eyes, which is another way to ensure their employment.

It's important to note that while some roles become outdated, other opportunities open up, especially with parts that focus on managing AI systems and working alongside them. These positions often require different skill sets, such as system design, data analysis, and AI ethics management. There are loads of jobs sprouting up left and right thanks to AI and automation.

As mentioned, this is easier said than done for managers and leaders trying to balance automation benefits and an engaged workforce. A big part of this issue is how poorly managed transitions tend to be — especially when employees see their jobs at stake. Managers need to communicate changes, offer training or upskilling opportunities (if available), redefine job roles, if necessary (to make them more engaging), and even address emotional/psychological challenges brought on by these changes since creativity, problem-solving, and emotional intelligence aren't skills that AI has yet.

It's challenging to navigate the delicate tightrope between automation benefits and maintaining employee morale (especially when job cuts are involved). But it's necessary for long-term success and sustainability in a world seemingly becoming more automated.

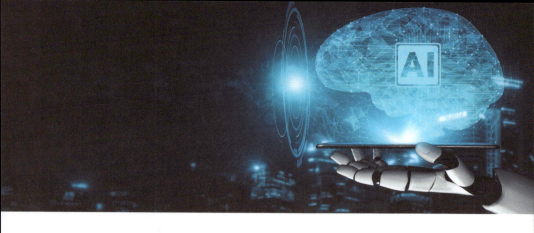

CHAPTER 10
THE MANAGER'S PERSPECTIVE

In Chapter 10, "The Manager's Perspective," we step into the polished shoes of managers navigating the brave new world of AI at the workplace. Picture this chapter as the ultimate 'Manager's Guide to AI,' minus the boring lectures and with a few more chuckles. It's for the leaders, the decision-makers, and anyone who's ever found themselves thinking, "So, I have this team, and now there's this AI thing. Help?"

We start with "Leading in the Age of AI," where we tackle the art of steering the ship in AI-infused waters. It's about being the captain who can navigate through the fog of technology without hitting an iceberg. This section is a mix of sage advice and practical tips, ensuring you don't accidentally turn your office into a scene from a sci-fi movie.

Next, in "AI for Decision Making: A Manager's Best Friend," we explore how AI can be the trusty sidekick for making more intelligent decisions. It's like having a crystal ball with data and algorithms instead of magic. This chapter is about leveraging AI to look like the most thoughtful person in the boardroom (even if you're faking it till you make it).

"Managing AI Teams: The Human Touch" delves into the nuances of leading a team where some members might be made of code rather than flesh and blood. It's about balancing human creativity with machine efficiency, ensuring your team doesn't feel like they're in an episode of "Westworld."

Next, we delve into 'AI and Organizational Change,' a manual for steering through the often turbulent process of integrating AI into your business. It's akin to being a technologically adept leader, navigating the vast ocean of digital transformation without succumbing to its challenges.

In "The Ethics of AI in Management," we put on our philosopher's hats and ponder the moral implications of AI in the workplace. This section is about ensuring your AI doesn't accidentally become a digital overlord but rather a force for good.

"Preparing Your Team for AI" is like a training montage for the digital age. It's about getting your team up to speed with AI, turning them from tech newbies into savvy operators who won't accidentally set off the AI equivalent of a kitchen fire.

"AI and the Future of Work" takes a crystal ball approach to what the workplace of tomorrow might look like. Will we all be working from hoverboards? Probably not, but AI is changing the game in ways we're just beginning to understand.

"The Role of Managers in an AI World" discusses how the manager's role is evolving in an AI-driven landscape. It's about being a guide, a mentor, and sometimes a referee in a world where humans and machines work side by side.

"AI and Employee Engagement" explores how AI can help keep your team happy, productive, and maybe even slightly excited about

Monday mornings. It's about using AI to create an efficient, engaging, enjoyable workplace.

Finally, "The Manager's AI Toolkit" arms you with the tools, tips, and tricks to make AI work for you, not against you. It's like having a Swiss Army knife for the digital age, ensuring you're prepared for whatever AI throws your way.

"The Manager's Perspective" is for the managers who find themselves at the helm in the age of AI, offering practical advice, ethical considerations, and a touch of humor. It's about leading confidently, navigating the challenges, and seizing the opportunities AI brings to the workplace. So, grab your managerial toolkit (and maybe a cup of AI-brewed coffee), and let's dive into the art of managing in AI.

81. Leading in the Age of AI - Leaders have to learn new skills in the fast-paced world of AI. Managers are now at the head of a technological army, and cooperating with the beast is critical to making it out in one piece. They need to learn how these systems work and how they can fit into their existing strategies. Doing this once isn't enough either; they must keep learning as AI evolves. Leaders also need to be ready for the consequences that come with AI. Data leaks and algorithmic bias can happen even if you think you're the hottest shot on the block.

Now that we have everything out, here's the real kicker: You can't just have technical skills. This kind of leadership requires more than just knowing how things work in theory. It also needs creative problem solvers who aren't afraid to fail. Team members must feel safe when they try new ideas, or no progress will be made. Leaders also must balance what's good for them and what's good for us as people. They have all this power at their fingertips, but they mustn't go overboard and use it recklessly or maliciously.

Being a leader nowadays means cultivating technical skills, innovation support, and ethical thinking. If they can mix these better, they will survive and lead team members through something revolutionary in both business and society.

82. **AI for Decision Making: A Manager's Best Friend** - The business world is seeing the importance of AI more and more today. Especially when it comes to managerial decision-making, the amount of data AI can process and analyze allows managers to make much better decisions. There's no doubt that this has been a game-changer for them. With these tools, they can make well-informed decisions about various parts of their business. This includes market trends, which are crucial for staying ahead of competitors. It also allows you to understand customer behavior, which is vital when tailoring products/services to meet customer needs.

AI's role in business doesn't just stop there, though. Practical applications can include predictive analytics, which helps companies to forecast market demand. Using this information, you can adjust inventory and production plans to avoid overproduction or stock shortages. Similarly, AI can be used to create optimal pricing strategies as well. By looking at market data, customer purchasing patterns, and competitor pricing, it can recommend pricing points that will help maximize profits while still keeping customers happy with the price.

Identifying inefficiencies in production processes is another one of its capabilities. This alone helps slash costs and improve operational efficiency quite significantly as well. For example, it might look at how your supply chain management currently works and suggest improvements that could be made.

While insights are great, it's also important to note that AI can help automate routine decision-making. By caring for the little things for managers, they can shift their focus onto more significant tasks that require human insight and creativity.

There's no denying it - adding AI into management practices has been huge for managers worldwide. It allows them to make better decisions with far more accuracy than ever before while leaving monotonous tasks for the intelligent systems instead.

83. **Managing AI Teams: The Human Touch -** Leading teams that are heavily involved in the development or application of AI is no easy task. Managers need to understand technology deeply, but that's not enough. This knowledge needs to be coupled with exceptional people skills. Not only do managers need to understand what AI is capable of and how it works, but they also need to understand its limitations. Without this knowledge, setting goals and expectations becomes incredibly difficult. In turn, teams can become frustrated if they are given unrealistic targets.

But there's more that goes into managing these types of teams than being knowledgeable in tech. Managers must ensure their team is well-rounded in terms of skillset. Tech competencies like data science and programming are a good foundation for any AI project, but it doesn't stop there. For example, an AI project in healthcare would benefit immensely from having team members with a background in medical science. This allows projects to adopt holistic approaches and develop technologically sound and practically relevant solutions.

Communication is vital when it comes to managing an AI-focused team, too. Bridging the gap between technical and non-technical stakeholders is a critical skill for anyone who leads one of these teams. Explaining complex concepts to someone with no technological background ensures that everyone involved understands the AI's capabilities, progress, and potential impact on productivity or safety risks.

An often overlooked aspect of managing teams like this is the ethical ramifications of working so closely with technology as powerful as AI. As it continues to grow at an unprecedented speed, its influence on society will continue to grow, too. To ensure we're heading in the right direction, we'll need stringent ethical guidelines and best practices for all types of projects involving AI. Leaders must foster an ethical culture within their teams.

Leading teams like these requires a different kind of leader than most other fields. Managers must be deeply ingrained in the tech and capable of assembling and nurturing a multi-skilled team. Writing this off as another management position can be disastrous for the project and the company.

84. AI and Organizational Change - Implementing AI within an organization is transformative. It goes beyond just upgrading technology — it can fundamentally change workflows, redefine job roles, and reshape company culture. Managers play a critical role in this landscape of change. They're responsible for navigating the implementation of AI systems and managing the human aspects of this transition.

Technically speaking, implementing AI involves integrating AI systems into already existing workflows. Managers have to rethink and redesign processes with the new capabilities that AI has to offer. This isn't as simple as installing new software or hardware. Managers must work closely with IT teams and AI specialists to ensure that technology is implemented effectively. Which then aligns with the organization's goals. This is often done through trial and error, where systems are tested, feedback is collected, and adjustments are made. It's a complex task that requires patience, technical understanding, skill sets, and a clear vision of the end goal.

Just as important is managing the human aspect of AI implementation. A manager's people skills come into play here. They must ensure employees are adequately trained and prepared for the new ways they'll work with AI. This could involve training sessions, workshops, or even one-on-one coaching, depending on how complex the system is compared to how skilled your workforce currently is.

Ensuring employees feel comfortable working alongside AI will help make this transition go smoothly.

On top of this, managers must address any concerns or resistance employees might have about the implementation process. Employees tend to fear AI will replace their jobs, so it's natural for them to be apprehensive about AI.

Managers must communicate effectively by articulating clearly how AI is intended to enhance their work rather than replace it. This means demonstrating benefits, such as how AI can take over mundane tasks like data entry and focus more on creative work.

It would be best to foster an environment where employees' concerns are heard and addressed while ensuring that AI's benefits are transparent.

A manager's role in implementing AI is multifaceted and crucial. They must handle the technical aspects of AI integration while managing the human side of this transition. Employees must be comfortable with the new tech, and any concerns or resistance must be addressed. Navigating this challenge successfully will allow managers to lead their organizations through a smooth AI transformation, ensuring that its introduction catalyzes growth, efficiency, and innovation.

85. The Ethics of AI in Management - Navigating the ethical landscape of AI implementation in management is both super important and complex. As AI technology becomes more prominent in business operations, you must prioritize ethics when deploying it. Issues such as data privacy, bias in AI algorithms, and the impact of AI on employment aren't just theoretical concerns but real-life problems that have enormous implications for individuals and society.

Data privacy is a big concern, especially with how valuable data is today. It would be best to have your AI respect user privacy and implement strong data security measures that comply with regulations. It won't just be about keeping information safe; you'll also have to gain and keep your customers' trust. They and your employees are becoming more aware and concerned about how their data is being used/shared.

Another crucial issue is bias in AI algorithms. Since AI systems are built from training data, they can accidentally make existing preferences worse or create new ones. This means you'll have to actively look out for this stuff and do something about it. Solutions could range from using fairer algorithms or reviewing/adjusting systems regularly so you can fix imbalances. You'll have to do it since it is not only a technical challenge but also a moral imperative if you want fairness/equity with the decisions made by AI.

Now, let's talk about the impact of AI on employment. While there's no doubt that AI will make things faster/better while opening up new opportunities, we also can't ignore the fact that some people might lose their jobs because of it. When managing AI ethically, you'll want to avoid overlooking this topic and consider how you'll help employees transition into different roles or offer training for budding job opportunities within your company's new environment.

The last thing we should mention here is how it affects society. With every advancement in tech comes the fear that it'll divide us more than we already are. You have to consider this, too. When you deploy AI, ensure it does some good for society and doesn't burden certain groups.

Managing AI isn't just about the technical stuff. You have to ensure that everything is transparent and fair and respects the privacy of those who use it. It would be best if you also were quick in finding/addressing biases in your systems. There are many moving parts when it comes to managing AI ethically. Still, if you take them all into account, you can ensure that your organization and society benefit from it.

86. **Preparing Your Team for AI -** Getting your team ready to work alongside AI goes beyond just teaching them the technical stuff. Building up a team that is constantly learning and adapting is the name of the game in our ever-changing world with AI. And as their manager, it's your job to get them there. You're not only their teacher but their coach and biggest motivator.

First, you must give your team ways to learn about AI and develop the necessary skills. This means teaching them data literacy (essential for just about any field) and analytical thinking (which forms the foundation for understanding how to use AI). It would be best if you introduced plenty of different learning formats so you can cater to everyone on your team who has other ways of learning. You can set up formal training programs for those who prefer a more structured approach toward education. Workshops conducted by AI experts are great, too, because they provide practical experience and allow your team members to interact with professionals in the field. But let's not forget about self-guided learning! That's big, too, because signing up for online courses, webinars, or just reading materials lets each member of your team explore everything at their own pace and according to their own interests.

There are also non-traditional ways, like experimenting with AI on real projects, participating in hackathons, or partnering up with other teams in your organization who specialize in AI. Allowing hands-on experience with this technology will help them understand how it can be applied to what they do day-to-day.

After all that's said and done, we must remember that making room for errors is essential here. Learning doesn't happen without some bumps in the road, so it's crucial to encourage creativity and innovation by having an environment where they feel safe enough to test new ideas.

And don't forget to walk the walk either! Showing that you're committed as a leader to learning about AI will motivate your team to do the same. Sharing your experiences and what you've learned will also set the stage for a culture of collaboration and learning.

Long story short, turning your team into pros who can work with AI is a long journey that involves teaching them technical skills, helping them develop a mindset open to always learning new things, and letting them experiment on their own. Provide different ways they can learn, show them it's okay to make mistakes and lead by example!

87. AI and the Future of Work - As we chart a future of AI-shaped work, it's increasingly evident that monumental shifts and changes will define the terrain. The world will see a rise in automation, new jobs will come to be, and lifelong learning will become necessary. And with that context, managers are more crucial now than ever before. They are the navigators who must anticipate these changes and strategically steer their organizations to adapt and thrive in an AI-augmented workplace.

A large part of this task is simply identifying which tasks can effectively be automated within the organization. It's not about replacing human labor but optimizing it. Automation's main objective is to take over repetitive and monotonous tasks so that employees can focus on more critical areas that require human skills, such as creativity, problem-solving, and emotional intelligence. This shift can lead to more fulfilling work for employees and greater efficiency for the organization.

But automation also means that job roles need to be redefined. Looking into the future, we'll see new parts rise out of nowhere as existing ones evolve, requiring different technical skill sets. We need managers with foresight in redesigning these positions, emphasizing how human abilities can work hand-in-hand with AI systems, from integrating AI into creative processes to using AI-driven insights to enhance decision-making.

Crucial to all this change is reskilling and upskilling the workforce. The skills valued in an AI-driven future likely won't be what was valued in the past, so managers must invest heavily in their employee's continuous development. This could involve offering training programs in AI and related technologies while simultaneously focusing on developing soft skills or encouraging cross-functional learning. By ensuring employees have what it takes for future jobs, organizations secure their futures and show commitment toward their workforce's personal growth and job security.

On top of this, managers should also foster a culture where learning never stops within their organization. In such a rapidly changing world, the ability to learn and adapt becomes more valuable by the second. The key is encouraging employees to believe learning is an ongoing journey rather than a one-time event. This can be done by providing access to learning resources, setting aside time for learning activities, and even incentivizing development.

The future of AI work comes with massive changes, and managers have a crucial role in preparing for it. They must identify opportunities for automation, redefine job roles to emphasize human skills and invest in reskilling and upskilling their workforce. But above all else, they must cultivate a culture where learning never stops. With this mentality, managers can lead their teams into navigating and flourishing in the future AI-enhanced workplace.

88. **The Role of Managers in an AI World** - The landscape has shifted rapidly in an AI-driven world, demanding managerial roles that undergo a significant transformation. Automation is a component that will soon, and already has to an extent, be integrated into this line of work to automate the finite tasks that are usually a time-suck for managers. Artificial Intelligence (AI) technology has now taken over scheduling, data analysis, and reporting. But don't worry, managers still hold importance in this new system. Their work has shifted to what only humans can do — things AI could never replace.

It's the human aspects of management: empathy, effective communication, and ethical leadership skills. They're becoming more critical every day. Managers can now concentrate less on simple tasks and more on their teams. Understanding and responding to each team member's needs, motivations, and concerns requires empathy. This skill is crucial when AI handles routine task management.

Effective communication becomes priority number one as managers serve as a bridge between humans and AI systems. Ensuring everyone understands organizational goals and AI initiatives while aligning with them may seem simple, but it's far from simple.

Ethical leadership is another aspect top-tier managers must balance as well. Integrating AI systems into business operations brings new dilemmas like privacy concerns or biases in AI systems. It's on the manager to navigate these problems thoughtfully so they're used in a way that benefits everyone involved.

Building and leading effective teams is yet another hurdle for these managers to conquer — especially now with added complexity due to the rise of automation allegedly making human jobs irrelevant. These leaders must assemble a proper mix of skills, but they'll also have to foster innovation and teach their team how to learn continuously. Only then will organizations keep up with agility and their actual competition.

AI will make businesses grow efficiently alongside organizations, but it isn't all good news either, as both sides must consider societal impacts. Managers have to advocate for responsible AI use. If we don't, they'll find us in a position where job displacement and ethical use of AI are far from balanced.

Managers must evolve in this new world from focusing on task management (because AI takes care of that now) to human elements of leadership. Empathy, communication, and ethical leadership must be developed, diverse and innovative teams built, and AI must be used to benefit organizations and the society they function within.

89. **AI and Employee Engagement** - The potential for AI to revolutionize employee engagement is vast. It offers dimensions and insights into worker satisfaction that we've never seen before. From employee surveys to daily interactions, these AI tools can analyze various data points to provide a comprehensive view of the workforce's morale and engagement. This insight is invaluable because it allows managers to identify areas of concern even if they're not immediately visible.

AI's ability to personalize the employee's experience also marks a significant advancement in engagement. After an employee joins, AI can tailor the onboarding process to their learning style and needs. As their career progresses, AI can recommend training programs, suggest different paths, and even show skill gaps that need bridging. Essentially, this will make the employee feel more engaged, enhancing overall happiness with work.

But while AI has many benefits regarding increasing worker satisfaction, managers should also be aware of its drawbacks. The introduction of AI into any workplace can be met with a hostile reception. Employees may feel threatened by its presence, fearing becoming redundant or being monitored excessively. To avoid this unnecessary stress from employees, transparently communicate its purpose and ensure that it's meant to help employees do their jobs better, not replace them.

Lastly, make sure that you're using AI ethically and responsibly. This involves being transparent about how it collects data and ensuring employees' privacy is continually respected. Doing this will reassure workers that their best interest is at heart.

AI offers new ways to enhance employee engagement. Still, success relies on managers being mindful of what problems could arise once implemented in any scenario involving humans dependent on their jobs for money or stability.

90. **The Manager's AI Toolkit** - The ability to manage in an AI-driven environment is complex. It's full of challenges and opportunities but requires robust skills and resources. Managers need to equip themselves with a variety of competencies if they want to stay ahead of the curve in business.

And even though it may seem intimidating, managing AI isn't impossible. The foundation needed is a basic understanding of AI technologies and their applications. That doesn't mean you have to become an expert, but having a solid grasp of concepts like machine learning, natural language processing, and robotics is more than good enough. Understand the potential and limitations of AI; this will help you make better decisions about integrating it into your business structure.

But it doesn't stop at understanding AI technologies alone - especially with data analysis becoming increasingly important. In an AI-driven environment, decisions are always going to be data-driven. With that said, managers must be able to interpret insights provided by AI systems effectively. This goes beyond just knowing how to understand numbers; you need to be able to translate these insights into actionable strategies for your business.

Moving on from data analysis, we have something much bigger — ethical and legal considerations surrounding AI. As you probably guessed, integrating AI into everyday business operations brings along complex moral issues such as data privacy and algorithmic bias, to name a couple. On top of that, we can't ignore the potential impact of AI on employment either — this will lead to its own set of problems.

You must also understand the legal landscape to avoid legal issues with your AI initiatives. This includes regulations related to both AI and data use.

Luckily, many resources are available for managers looking to enhance their skills. Online courses are a good start when looking for ways to learn about everything related to tech (AI). Industry reports & journals can keep you updated with the latest trends and best practices. Lastly, experimenting with AI tools and software can give you the hands-on experience to make proper decisions.

Many platforms today offer trial versions or user-friendly interfaces that allow managers to explore AI functionalities. It's a great way to consider how they might be applied in business operations.

In short, managing in an AI-driven environment isn't easy — far from it. But it isn't impossible either. Equip yourself with diverse skills and resources to thrive in this landscape. A basic understanding of AI technologies, data analysis proficiency, and ethical/legal familiarity are fundamental. With the help of online courses, industry reports, and AI tools — you'll have everything necessary to lead your team through an increasingly tech-centered world.

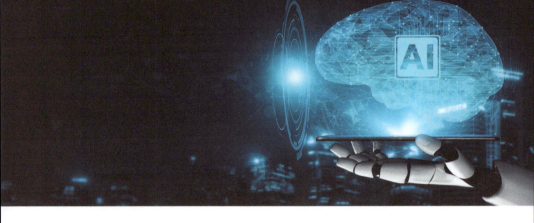

CHAPTER 11
PERSONAL ANECDOTES AND INSIGHTS

Chapter 11, "Personal Anecdotes and Insights," is where we take a break from all the tech talk and get personal with AI. Think of it as sitting around a digital campfire, sharing stories about our adventures and misadventures with Artificial Intelligence (AI). It's less about the nuts and bolts of AI and more about the heart and soul – with a sprinkle of humor, because who says AI can't be fun?

We start with "My First Encounter with AI," where we reminisce about our first dates with AI. Maybe it was love at first sight with a smartphone assistant or an awkward introduction to a smart home device with a mind of its own. These stories are like AI baby photos – cute, endearing, and embarrassing.

Next, in "AI Fails: Humorous Blunders," we share those facepalm moments where AI didn't quite get it right. From autocorrect disasters that turned innocent texts into comedy gold to GPS navigations that led us astray, this section reminds us that AI, like humans, has its 'oops' moments.

"AI Success Stories: Small Victories" celebrates the wins, big and small, in our journey with AI. It's like a highlight reel of those times when AI made us look like geniuses at work or saved the day at home. These stories are the high-fives and pats on the back we give AI for a well-done job.

In "Lessons Learned from Implementing AI," we reflect on the wisdom gained from our experiences with AI. It's like gathering the nuggets of truth from our trials and triumphs and turning them into valuable life (and tech) lessons. Spoiler alert: it involves a lot of trial and error and a bit of patience.

"The Human Impact of AI" takes a thoughtful look at how AI changes how we live, work, and interact. It's about the people behind the screens and algorithms and how this tech wave is more than just ones and zeros – it's about human stories.

"AI in My Daily Routine" is a sneak peek into our everyday lives with AI. From morning alarms to workout routines, it's about the small ways AI has become our digital sidekick. It's like having a personal assistant who's always on but doesn't need coffee breaks.

In "The Future I Hope for with AI," we dream big and share our hopes for what AI might bring to our world. It mixes optimistic visions and sci-fi fantasies with a touch of realism. Think flying cars, but also more competent healthcare and more sustainable living.

"AI Misconceptions I Had" is where we confess our initial misunderstandings about AI. Did we think robots would be doing our laundry by now? Maybe. This section is about debunking myths and setting the record straight, with a chuckle or two.

"The Most Surprising Thing About AI" reveals our AI journey's unexpected twists and turns. It's about those 'aha' moments that left us amazed (or baffled) at what AI can do. Spoiler: it's not just about robots.

Lastly, "AI and the Balance of Work and Life" explores how AI reshapes work-life balance. It's about finding harmony in a world where our colleagues might be algorithms and our personal assistants digital.

"Personal Anecdotes and Insights" of "Bots & Brilliance" is a heartwarming, sometimes hilarious, and always insightful collection of personal AI tales. It's a reminder that AI is a part of our human story at the end of the day – and it's one heck of a tale to tell. So, grab some marshmallows for that digital campfire, and let's share some AI stories.

91. **My First Encounter with AI -** "Siri's Off-Key Opera": It was a brisk autumn evening in 2015. I decided to see the fuss and give Siri, the latest iPhone assistant, a spin. Hugging my iPhone 6s – a gadget that looked like it beamed down from the Starship Enterprise – I said: "Hello, Siri."

"Good evening! How can I help you today?" Siri responded with a voice that was somehow both robotically cheerful and digitally warm.

Feeling cheeky, I asked: "Siri, can you sing me a song?" I expected her to say no or instead tell me a joke.

There was a brief, suspenseful pause. Then Siri began to sing. Not quite melodic but more monotone. It is a tune that might charm an accountant but not quite make it for humans. My honest reaction was to burst into laughter — charmed by the earnest yet tuneless effort.

That night, Siri went from just another button on my phone to my new off-key robotic pal. It marked my first dance with AI, and it wasn't precisely graceful — more of a clumsy stomp than anything else.

Looking back at how infatuated I was by such a simple interaction is amusing now. Nowadays, AI is as complicated as it gets. Still, something about my first encounter with Siri makes me smile — it's like wonderment and giggles dancing hand in hand with each other right into the future, where technology tried so hard to stay in tune but somehow always slipped up just enough to keep things interesting.

92. **AI Fails Humorous Blunders** - "The Feline Fiasco": The day my AI shopping assistant decided I was a cat person was when I learned two things: First, that it had a sense of humor; second, that sometimes it got things really, hilariously wrong.

The app's creators claimed it was powered by Artificial Intelligence (AI) so advanced that it could deduce my needs and wants with almost psychic accuracy. And to be fair, until that point, the app had done nothing but wow me with its algorithmic prowess. But then, out of nowhere, my new brilliant best friend recommended cat food, which would have been fine — if I owned a cat.

Amused by this glitch in the matrix, I tapped on the recommendation. It took me to a whole page of different options for feeding imaginary Mr. Whiskers at 7 p.m. or whenever cats eat dinner these days. And as I scrolled through all the fancy choices, from salmon pâté to chicken chunks (all available for subscription!), I couldn't help but laugh. What a life old Whiskers must lead inside my mind!

This little hiccup reminded me that even with all their data-crunching and pattern-predicting power, AIs like this one can still leap to hilariously fantastical conclusions — just like any well-meaning but haplessly misguided human friend who keeps setting you up on terrible dates. The only thing missing was a message from Mr. Whiskers himself.

But even though this little feline fiasco didn't end with me adding cat food to my cart (I swear), it did succeed in making AIs seem more approachable and less intimidating. Because if something as bright as this can have its "oops" moments, we probably shouldn't worry too much about what our microchips might get wrong.

93. AI Success Stories: Small Victories - "My Spanish Saga with a Digital Don Quixote": My encounter with a language app was like a comedy of blunders, with me playing the central role of the oblivious linguist. I had always been to languages what a fish is to a bicycle – utterly useless. But then, I downloaded this AI-powered language learning app, my very own digital Don Quixote, ready to conquer the windmills of Spanish grammar and vocabulary.

The app was kind yet robotic. It listened to me fail at speaking tongue twisters and offered corrections with the enthusiasm of a toaster – it got the job done but didn't seem too excited about it. Each session was a mix of triumphs and word tangles, making my language-learning journey feel like dancing while tripping on marbles.

Then came the day of reckoning. I found myself in a local Mexican restaurant, armed with my newfound linguistic skills. The waiter's expression said it all: he thought I sounded ridiculous. But then he complimented my accent and effort before we started chatting briefly in Spanish. As I walked away, feeling like I just won an Olympic gold medal in language gymnastics, all that kept ringing in my ears was his smiley "¡Adios!" as if he understood me perfectly fine.

This experience showed me that AI can teach an old dog new tricks, even with bumps. It wasn't just about learning Spanish; it was about embracing the hilarity of learning anything new through

AI software. The app didn't just teach me a language; it gave me confidence, laughter, and... ... this story! This digital Don Quixote made for one good partner on a quest for bilingual banter.

94. **Lessons Learned from Implementing AI -** "The Chronicles of the Gardening Bot": I thought implementing an AI system for my small garden at home would be a good idea. The objective was to have a paradise easily maintained by intelligent technology. To do this, I purchased an AI-powered gardening bot that could water and monitor plant health. I was bringing the future to my backyard!

The first few days were a dream come true! Sprouts were growing from the ground, and plants were being watered evenly. However, the challenges started rolling in soon after. The bot couldn't distinguish between my flowers and the weeds taking over my yard. It did what it knew best – water everything equally.

This is where I learned that you can't just throw AI at something and expect it to work without problems. You need to make sure your data is vital, as well as implementing clear objectives. Lastly, you must understand that AI isn't human – it doesn't have judgment or intervention as we do.

Though not entirely successful, this project taught me so much. It opened my eyes to how vital exemplary implementation is when using AI in any project or task. Sure, the bot didn't create my perfect garden, but it planted some seeds on how I should apply AI next time!

95. **The Human Impact of AI -** "The Culinary Adventures of Anna and Marco": A compelling tale in a small town where traditional cooking and innovative tech collide in a fascinating cooking competition. It wasn't just a showcase of skills and proof that Artificial Intelligence (AI) can transform everyday life.

With her tech-savvy brain, Anna used AI for everything at her restaurant. The hub of innovation managed inventory analyzed food trends, and perhaps the most staggering use of it all was the creation of personalized menus for each visitor. And people loved it!

Dining there was an experience. People wondered if Anna's AI could guess what they wanted to eat based on their mood. This fusion of technology and food made her restaurant a place to eat and a destination to see the future.

On the other hand, Marco — who owned the kitchen next door — only wanted simplicity. A purist at heart. His pots and pans were old-fashioned, and his belief in the human touch never wavered, even in today's age of technology.

At first, people seemed to enjoy his soufflés more than ever while Anna's restaurant began emptying daily. But as time passed, it became evident that Marco's stubbornness was costing him customers... Many visitors preferred eating at Anna's because, just like them, she embraced modernity.

As days passed, one thing became evident: The two restaurants were on two different paths... Anna's was born into success thanks to the implementation of AI, while Marco's empty seats started becoming more noticeable... And let me tell you... That silence? It clung onto your eardrums.

This tells us how AI has bulldozed our lives like a bull into a China shop... Reshaping industries and altering destinies along the way, too!

Anna embraced this new wave head-on and rode it to success while Marco tried holding onto his ways of old... Which left him struggling against the relentless march of progress.

But as we look back at the story and reminisce on Marco's old-fashioned soufflés, one thing becomes apparent: We've lost sight of the balance between tradition and innovation.

96. AI in My Daily Routine - "A Day in the Life with My AI Sidekick": Picture us as a comedic pair. My AI companion and I keep the laughter flowing all day. It starts with my not-so-ordinary coffee maker, an AI marvel, preparing a brew so potent it could rouse a hibernating bear amidst its bubbling and hissing. Then, as if that's not lively enough, my smart speaker jumps in, blasting music like I'm on an intense caffeine high.

But there's more! My fitness app transforms into a no-nonsense coach, reminding me to stretch regularly. It's like having a personal trainer, minus the high-fives and pep talks. And when the workday, which seems endless, finally wraps up, it's time for the evening spectacle.

This means transforming my home into a serene sanctuary with a single voice command. The lighting softens, mimicking a sunset right in my living room. Living here is akin to starring in a futuristic film in a spaceship I call home.

Thankfully, this AI ally simplifies everything, even those startling moments like accidentally stumbling over my cat in the dark.

I add the human element throughout the day, while AI takes care of the rest. We resemble a sitcom duo, navigating daily life with humor and brilliance in our unique ways.

97. The Future I Hope for with AI - "The AI Orchestra: No Conductor Required" My hope for AI's future is like dreaming of an orchestra where the instruments tune themselves, and the musicians show up just in time for a flawless performance. In this symphony, AI isn't the authoritative conductor; it's more like the unsung hero who makes sure everyone's sheet music isn't upside down.

I imagine a world where AI tackles the heavy notes of climate change, analyzing weather patterns like a meteorological Mozart. It could play a tune that predicts storms precisely and makes weather forecasters look like amateur kazoo players.

In healthcare, AI could be the virtuoso violinist, playing harmonies in medical research and helping to compose personalized treatment opuses for patients. It's like having a doctor who's also a diagnostic DJ, spinning data into health insights.

And let's not forget the arts. AI could collaborate with human artists, creating a fusion genre that's part classical, part techno, and entirely groundbreaking. It's like pairing Beethoven with beatboxing or Picasso with pixel art.

Most importantly, I dream of an AI future that's inclusive and ethical, where AI tools don't play favorites. It's a world where technology is like a community orchestra, open to all, playing a tune that benefits the entire neighborhood.

AI and humans co-create a harmonious, innovative, and whimsical future in this symphony of minds. It's a reminder that the future of AI should have us all tapping our feet, ready to dance along to the rhythm of progress.

98. **AI Misconceptions I Had -** "The Day My Toaster Didn't Take Over the World": Once upon a time, I half-thought I might wake up to a world run by robots, like something out of 'Rise of the Toasters.' There was just something about how smart tech had gotten that made me think we were on the brink of being bossed around by AI. It even crossed my mind that they'd have us make our coffee.

This 'toaster take over' notion grew more robust as more sci-fi movies emerged. That is until I went to a tech seminar at university. This was my chance to learn how to stay on our future robot overlords' good side. Or so I thought.

What happened instead was quite a reality check. AI isn't about plotting world domination but figuring out which pictures are of cats and which are of dogs. See, it's less scheming genius and a more excellent calculator. One that still needs someone to press the buttons, at least.

Learning this was equal parts comforting and disappointing — well, mostly frustrating. After all, what would I do with all those hours spent perfecting my 'I, for one, welcome our new robot overlords' speech?

But in all seriousness, this experience did teach me something: AI might be super smart, but it's not here to replace humanity. Just ask any cyber security company if you don't believe me.

All my toaster wants is an English Muffin — and I must keep making them every morning.

99. **The Most Surprising Thing About AI -** "When AI Went to Art School": The day I discovered AI could be artsy was when my whole 'robots-are-just-for-numbers' view got a paint-splattered makeover. I always thought of AI as the class nerd, great with equations and data but not someone you'd expect to see at a poetry slam or an art show.

Then, I stumbled upon an art exhibition featuring AI-generated pieces. It felt like walking into a gallery curated by a computer with a flair for the dramatic. Each artwork was a wild mix of colors and shapes, like a toddler's finger-painting session, but with a PhD in computational creativity.

This was far from my image of AI as a cold, calculating machine. Here it was, churning out art that made you tilt your head and squint, wondering if there was a deeper meaning or if the AI sneezed out colors randomly.

This artsy side of AI opened up my eyes. It wasn't just crunching numbers; it was creating beauty, or at least its silicon-chip version of it. Imagine finding out your accountant could moonlight as a jazz musician — that's what this felt like. This experience made me realize that AI could cross the line from logical to creative, blurring the boundaries between binary and brushstrokes.

It reminded me that AI's potential is as vast and unpredictable as a canvas waiting for its first stroke. And while I'm still not sure if AI will ever understand the subtle art of perfectly timed sarcasm, I can't wait for its next art show.

100. AI and the Balance of Work and Life - "My AI Assistant: The Never-Sleeping, Over-Eager Intern": When I first welcomed an AI assistant into my life, I imagined it would be like having a super-efficient, slightly robotic butler. Instead, I got more like an overzealous intern who never sleeps and is obsessed with organizing my life.

In the beginning, it was a dream. My AI assistant kept my calendar so organized I could've mistaken it for a military operation. It sorted my emails with the precision of a librarian on a sugar rush, and my productivity soared like a caffeinated eagle.

But then, the lines between work and personal life started to blur. With its constant pings and AI-driven nudges, my phone turned into a digital leash. It was like having a tiny boss in my pocket, reminding me of all-hour meetings, nudging me to check emails during dinner, and being a buzzkill at parties.

I realized the challenge wasn't the technology but how I used it. Setting boundaries became my new mantra. I had to teach my ever-eager AI assistant that while I appreciated its enthusiasm, it needed to chill out after 6 PM: no more reminders, sneak-peek emails, just peace.

This experience taught me that while AI can be a fantastic tool for efficiency, managing it is a bit like training a puppy – you need to set the rules, or it'll chew through your work-life balance. Now, I enjoy the perks of my AI assistant without letting it turn me into a workaholic robot. It's a partnership where I'm still the boss, and my AI intern gets some much-needed virtual sleep.

CONCLUSION:

101. **Embracing AI: A Call to Action** - Our deep dive into the vast and ever-changing Artificial Intelligence (AI) world has ended. One thing is sure: AI is more than a flashy fad in technology; its salvation is incarnate. The effect that AI has on society is impossible to ignore, as our journey revealed. Not only does it have endless applications across many different industries, but Artificial Intelligence (AI) brings ethical and societal issues alongside its rapid growth. We must be careful when embracing this new age of advancement and innovation. Innovation must be driven by progression and efficiency while keeping a keen eye on all the challenges that come with it.

The future holds much more AI in our lives than now, so we'll need to get ahead as soon as possible. It doesn't matter if you own a business or work for one, even if you're someone who has no idea what they're doing —if you want to grow your knowledge about this field, then we can help with that! There are countless ways in which integrating AI into your daily life will increase productivity, spark creativity, and boost your decision-making skills. However, these demands require you to keep up with the fast-paced evolution of AI and adapt your mindset around it.

The future of AI development is mostly in our hands, so it's up to us to guide and apply Artificial Intelligence (AI) responsibly within ethical boundaries that champion practices pushing for inclusive advancements while ensuring the benefits reach all levels regarding society's strata. This also includes evaluating how massively it will impact job markets and focusing on reskilling and upskilling initiatives so transitions can be easy as we cross into new territories created by AI.

In addition, AI's ability to collaborate must not be overlooked. The true power behind Artificial Intelligence (AI) isn't found in its capability to replace humans but in enhancing every fiber within them. Complex problems can be tackled more effectively when connected to humans at work. Whether it's climate change, medical breakthroughs, or solving other global challenges, it doesn't matter.

As we continue to integrate AI into the fabric of our existence, let us approach it with optimism and responsibility. Technological progress should never stray far from efficiency and productivity, but there must also be an equal focus on equity and justice. We still have a long way to go on our journey through AI, so let's stay diligent in learning, adapting, and innovating to make AI a force for positive transformation and progress.

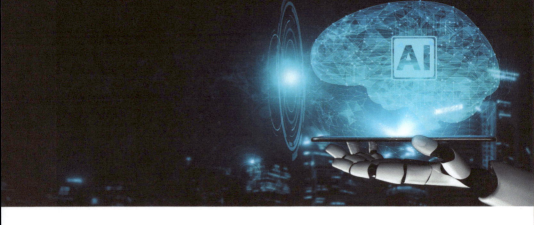

EPILOGUE:
NAVIGATING THE AI HORIZON

As we close the final pages of "Bots & Brilliance," let us pause and take a moment to reflect on the journey we have embarked on together. Through the chapters of this book, we have traversed the vast and intricate landscape of Artificial Intelligence (AI), uncovering its many facets, potentials, and challenges. We have seen how AI, once a concept confined to science fiction, has become an indelible part of our daily lives and a pivotal force in shaping our future.

But what does this journey through AI mean for us — as individuals, professionals, and members of a global society? The answer lies in understanding that our engagement with AI is not just about leveraging technology but about shaping a future. In all its complexity and wonder, AI is still just a tool crafted by human hands and minds. And so, we must navigate its path with intentionality, foresight, and profound responsibility.

As we stand at this juncture — looking towards a horizon where AI will play an even more significant role — we are reminded of the dual nature of technology: it is both an enabler of opportunities and a bearer of challenges. Advancements in algorithms and computing power will not just decide the future of AI. It will be shaped by the choices that we make as a society. It calls for a collaborative effort where policymakers, technologists, ethicists, and citizens come together to ensure that AI grows in alignment with our values, enhances our capabilities responsibly, and works towards the greater good.

The journey through AI is like sailing through uncharted waters — full of excitement, possibilities, uncertainties, and risks. As we sail forward, let's carry the lessons learned from each insight shared in this book. Let's continue questioning things around us, learning from them, innovating new approaches, listening to varying perspectives, empathizing with others, and caring for one another. After all, the future of AI is not just about what more we can do but also about who we are becoming.

Ultimately, "Bots & Brilliance" is not just a book about AI. It is an invitation to a conversation, a journey, a collective effort to harness the power of AI with wisdom, ethics, and a vision for a better world. As we turn the last page, know this — the story of AI is far from over. It's only just the beginning. And it's one that each one of us has a share in writing.

So let's step forward then — with hope and determination — ready to shape, guide, and experience the future of AI together.

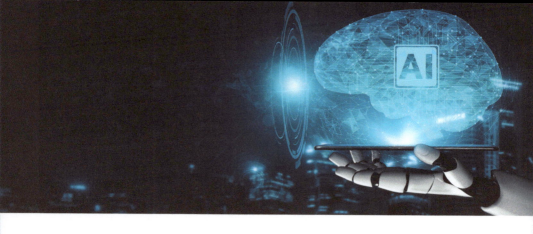

APPENDIX
KEY TERMS AND DEFINITIONS

Here are 50 key terms related to Artificial Intelligence (AI) accompanied by their definitions:

- **Activation Function**: A function in a Neural Network that defines the output of a neuron given a set of inputs.

- **Artificial General Intelligence (AGI):** A type of Artificial Intelligence (AI) that can understand, learn, and apply knowledge in a wide variety of tasks at a level comparable to human intelligence.

- **Algorithm**: A set of rules or procedures programmed into a computer to solve specific problems or accomplish a task.

- **Artificial Intelligence (AI):** The science of creating machines capable of performing tasks that usually require human intelligence.

- **Attention Mechanism**: A component in Neural Networks, particularly transformers, allows the model to focus on specific parts of the input data.

- **Autoencoder**: A Neural Network used for unsupervised learning of efficient encodings, often for dimensionality reduction or anomaly detection.

- **Backpropagation**: A training method used for adjusting the weights of neurons based on the error rate of the output.

- **Bagging**: An ensemble method that involves training multiple instances of the same model on different subsets of the data.

- **Batch Size**: The number of training examples utilized in one iteration.

- **Bias in Machine Learning (ML)**: Unwanted and often systematic discrepancies in data or algorithm outputs can lead to unfair or discriminatory results.

- **Boosting**: An ensemble method that trains models sequentially, each trying to correct its predecessor's mistakes.

- **ChatGPT**: A model by OpenAI that uses Generative Pre-trained Transformers (GPT) to simulate human-like conversation.

- **Clustering**: An unsupervised learning technique to group similar data points based on specific features.

- **Convolutional Neural Network (CNN)**: A Deep Learning algorithm primarily used for image processing and recognition.

- **Data Augmentation**: Techniques used to increase the amount of training data, like rotating or cropping images.

- **Deep Learning**: A subset of Machine Learning (ML) utilizing multiple layers of Neural Networks to analyze different data factors.

- **Decision Trees**: Supervised learning models used for classification and regression, representing decisions as branches.

- **Embeddings**: Representations of discrete data, like words, in continuous vector space, enabling mathematical operations.

- **Ensemble Methods**: Techniques combining multiple models' decisions to improve overall performance, such as bagging or boosting.

- **Epoch**: One complete forward and backward pass of all the training data through a Neural Network.

- **Feature Extraction**: The process of selecting or transforming variables from raw data to better model the underlying patterns.

- **Fine-tuning**: Adjusting a pre-trained model to a new task by further training it on recent data.

- **Generative Adversarial Network (GAN)**: A type of Neural Network setup where two networks, the generator and discriminator, are trained simultaneously through adversarial processes.

- **Gradient Descent**: An optimization algorithm used to minimize the value of the loss function by adjusting model parameters.

- **Hyperparameter**: Parameters set before training a Machine Learning (ML) model, like learning rate or batch size.

- **Inference Engine**: The component of an Artificial Intelligence (AI) system that applies logic rules to knowledge, drawing new conclusions.

- **Learning Rate**: A hyperparameter determines the step size at each iteration while moving towards a minimum in the loss function.

- **Loss Function**: A method of evaluating how well an algorithm models the given data. A lower value indicates a better fit.

- **Machine Learning (ML)**: A branch of Artificial Intelligence (AI) where computers learn from data to improve performance without explicitly being programmed for specific tasks.

- **Natural Language Processing (NLP)**: The intersection of Artificial Intelligence (AI) and linguistics that enables machines to understand, interpret, and produce human language.

- **Neural Network**: Computational structures inspired by the human brain's neurons, designed to recognize patterns from data.

- **Overfitting**: When a Machine Learning (ML) model tailors itself too closely to training data, performing poorly on unfamiliar data.

- **Perceptron**: A binary classification algorithm and a type of artificial neuron in Neural Network architecture.

- **Principal Component Analysis (PCA)**: A method for reducing data dimensionality while retaining as much variability as possible.

- **Random Forest**: An ensemble method that creates a 'forest' of decision trees and outputs the mode of the classes or means prediction.

- **Recurrent Neural Network (RNN)**: Neural Networks are designed to recognize patterns in data sequences, such as time series or natural language.

- **Regularization**: Techniques to prevent overfitting by adding penalties to the loss function.

- **Reinforcement Learning**: Machine Learning (ML) technique where algorithms learn by taking actions and receiving rewards or penalties based on those actions.

- **Semantics**: In Artificial Intelligence (AI) and Natural Language Processing (NLP), this refers to the study of meaning in language.

- **Sequence-to-Sequence Models**: Neural architectures designed for tasks where input and output sequences can be of different lengths, standard in translation or summarization.

- **Supervised Learning**: Machine Learning (ML) method where the model is trained using both input data and its corresponding correct output.

- **Support Vector Machine (SVM)**: A supervised Machine Learning (ML) algorithm that can be used for both classification and regression challenges.

- **Tokenization**: The process of converting text into individual elements or "tokens" for processing, usually in Natural Language Processing (NLP).

- **Transfer Learning**: Leveraging a pre-trained model on a new related task, saving training time and resources.

- **Transformer Architecture**: A Neural Network design often used in Natural Language Processing (NLP) tasks, introducing the attention mechanism to weigh input data differently.

- **Turing Test**: An evaluation of a machine's ability to exhibit intelligent behavior indistinguishable from a human.

- **Underfitting**: When a model is too simple to capture underlying patterns in the data.

- **Unsupervised Learning**: Machine Learning (ML) method where the algorithm identifies patterns in data without referring to known or labeled outcomes.

- **Validation Data**: Data used to fine-tune model parameters and prevent overfitting during training.

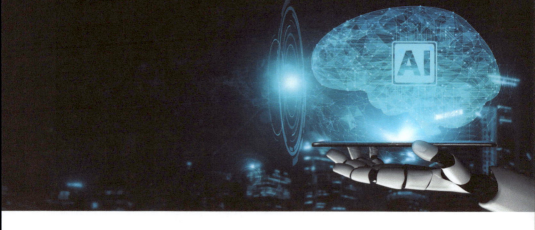

ACKNOWLEDGMENTS:

In the grand tradition of authors who have penned words that changed the world – or at least made it chuckle softly while nodding thoughtfully – I find myself at the daunting task of acknowledging those who have made *"Bots & Brilliance: 101 Things You Should Know About Artificial Intelligence"* less of a daydream and more of a thing you can actually drop on your foot.

Firstly, to my son Austin, whose tech-savviness and practical use of AI saved this manuscript from becoming a series of unfortunate digital accidents – your blend of patience and cheerful, excited encouragement has been a constant guide. Remember, without you, this book might have been handwritten!

Kelsey, my daughter, thank you for enduring AI talk over dinner and for your uncanny ability to nod thoughtfully even when I rambled about algorithms. Your subtle eye-rolling did not go unnoticed. Your ability to listen to me ramble about the existential implications of AI while simultaneously updating your social media is nothing short of a modern miracle. You're the real MVP.

Ah, and then there are my grandsons, Axel and Tommy. You two are living proof that the future is in good (albeit sticky) hands. Your boundless energy and curious minds remind me why understanding AI is crucial.

I must also tip my hat to my Coke Zero and Red Bull, tireless companions through the wee hours. You, dear friend, are the unsung heroes of this literary journey. Your steadfast supply of caffeine has fueled more chapters than I care to admit.

And to you, dear reader, for picking up this book. Whether you did it because of a deep interest in Artificial Intelligence (AI) or thought it was a new installment in a sci-fi series, I thank you. Your curiosity and willingness to dive into the world of AI is what makes all the late nights and caffeine-induced jitters worth it.

Here's to the future – may it be as bright and brilliant as we dare to imagine, and may our robots be friendly and our understanding of them profound. Cheers!

With warm regards and a hint of digital whimsy,

- John Binks

SHARE YOUR THOUGHTS:

We always appreciate feedback from our readers. Here's how you can reach out:

- General Feedback: For any inquiries or comments about this book, please email John@BotsAndBosses.com. Remember to include the book's title in your email's subject line.

- Errata: Despite our efforts to ensure content accuracy, errors can occur. If you spot a mistake, kindly inform us at John@BotsAndBosses.com. Your assistance is highly valued.

- Piracy: Should you encounter unauthorized copies of our work online, we'd be thankful if you could report the specific location or website to John@BotsAndBosses.com.

- Reviews: After reading "Bots & Brilliance: 101 Things You Should Know About Artificial Intelligence," we'd be delighted to hear your opinions. Please leave a review on Amazon and share your thoughts.

- Exclusive Offers: For special discounts, newsletters, and event information, visit our website at www.BotsAndBosses.com